Success with

Orchids

HALINA HEITZ

Series Editor

LESLEY YOUNG

MEREHURST

Contents

Phalaenopsis hybrids may flower two or three times in succession on the same shoot.

A single flower of Cymbidium "Vanguard".

Oncidium kramerianum from Peru.

Introduction

Contrary to popular belief, orchids are astonishingly adaptable and not nearly as difficult to grow as most people think, so if you have always had a desire to grow these enchanting indoor plants, throw caution to the winds and have a go. There is a huge range of splendid orchids to choose from, many of which will flourish on your windowsill just as well as African violets and other houseplants. Also, do not forget that, thanks to the ingenuity of breeders in raising new varieties, orchids are now less expensive than ever before and the great variety of shapes and colours can hardly fail to satisfy every wish and whim.

This full colour guide tells you about the important points of orchid care. In this text, experienced gardener Halina Heitz provides all the basic knowledge necessary for the successful care of orchids on windowsills and elsewhere indoors. Using clear, detailed instructions which are easy to follow even for a beginner, she explains what to look for when purchasing orchids, what range of temperatures orchids demand and how you can coax orchids to flourish and produce blooms on a windowsill with the minimum of fuss or expenditure. The exotic flower is, of course, the main aim of successful orchid care and, to this end, the author offers a range of useful advice and handy tips which will ensure that your orchids continue to flower every year. This includes advice about the optimum amount of light, humidity, water and nutrients and being aware of the right moment for the plants' dormant seasons. To make things even easier and to help you to develop a flair for growing orchids, this text also includes a section of individual plant descriptions with detailed instructions for care and advice on species and hybrids that are particularly suited to growing indoors. This section includes excellent colour photographs which may tempt keen orchid enthusiasts to grow a large selection of orchids on their windowsill.

Even with the best care, however, pests and diseases cannot be avoided all the time, so a section has been included to deal with this subject and to cover all the important points of prevention, identification and control of problems. Biological pest control methods are also discussed. Finally, if you develop orchid-growing fever to the extent that you want to begin propagating your own orchids, you will find detailed instructions on how to do this too. Its easy-to-follow, clear instructions, fine colour photographs (most of which were specially taken for this volume) and numerous excellent colour illustrations render this introduction to the world of orchid care an easy one and will provide many new ideas even for the experienced orchid lover.

The author

Halina Heitz is editor of the well-known German gardening magazine *Mein Schöner Garten*, for which she also writes on indoor gardens.

Acknowledgements

The author and publishers wish to thank everyone involved in the production of this volume, especially Jörgen Stork and the other plant photographers for the particularly beautiful colour photographs and Ushie Dorner for her informative illustrations. Special thanks go to Emil Lückel, President of the Deutsche Orchideengesellschaft (German Orchid Society) for his expert advice.

Author's note

This volume deals with the care of orchids indoors and on windowsills. There is, as yet, no comprehensive data on the toxicity of different orchids, so you should make absolutely sure that children or domestic pets are unable to touch or eat parts of the plants as there is always a risk of danger to health. Contact with hairy orchids may cause skin complaints, so always wear gloves when handling these orchids.

Elegant and easy to care for
Phalaenopsis hybrids thrive in heated rooms. A splendid new cultivar is shown here.

All about orchids

In popular literature, orchids have always been seen as symbols of love, seeming to represent the qualities of both femme fatale and seducer, and have also attracted the interest of scent makers over many centuries. There can hardly be another plant that is as changeable and adaptable as the orchid which belongs to one of the youngest families of plants in the botanical classification system.

The orchid family

Orchids belong among the monocotyledon plants, along with similar "young" plants such as palms, bananas or *Araceae*, although orchids produce more fully developed flowers than these other plants. The orchid family, known to botany as *Orchidaceae*, includes about 750 genera, 10,000 to 30,000 species and more than 70,000 hybrids or cultivars. This means that orchids represent almost 10 per cent of all flowering plants. Exactly how many species there are is impossible to establish, even for botanists, as these very adaptable plants frequently cross-breed in the wild.

Where do orchids live in the wild?

With the exception of polar and desert regions, orchids are found growing wild in all climatic regions of the world. They can be found in the Mongolian tundra and even in Greenland in the vicinity of hot springs. Approximately 60 species are native to central Europe and about 150 species occur in North America. Several species grow in Mexico, Central America and especially South America which is an orchid paradise. However, the great majority of orchids are resident in Asia which is considered to be their orginal home. In South America, they can be encountered at all levels of vegetation: in tropical rainforest (up to 1,000 m/3,200 ft); in tropical mountain forests (1,000-2,000 m/3,200-6,400 ft); in cool, extremely humid cloud forests (2,000-3,000 m/6,400-9,800 ft); and in rocky, coastal deserts facing the ocean, where a few species even grow at levels of 4,000 m/13,100 ft.

The curious life cycle of the orchid

Orchid growth is rather different from what we are accustomed to see in most garden or indoor plants. During the course of their evolution, they have had to adapt to constant change and many different environments and, as a result, have had to find their own "solutions" to each new challenge in order to survive in unfavourable positions. Just how adaptable this rather young family of plants is can be demonstrated by their many very different life forms.
Terrestrial orchids (from Latin *terra* = ground, soil) are rooted in soil. The European Green-winged Orchid (*Orchis morio*), for example, flourishes in loamy meadow soil that is rich in silicic acid, while the tropical lady's slipper orchids prefer a loose, humus-rich forest soil.
Epiphytes are the climbers within the family. In order to reach the light amid the prevailing gloom of the rainforest, they have adapted to living conditions in the tops of trees and in the forks of branches. Most of these epiphytes form aerial roots with which they cling on to their support and through which they also absorb nutrients and water. They are not, however, true parasites.
Lithophytes (from Greek *lithos* = stone) are a relatively small group which includes the stone *Laelia*. They flourish on bare rocks or extremely meagre layers of soil.

Typical shapes of growth

Orchids grow in two ways. They either extend their shoot tips, growing monopodially, or branch out laterally, growing sympodially. *In monopodial growth*, the new leaves always appear at the tip of the main axis. The plant seems to grow taller every year. The flowers appear along the main axis. There are no pseudo-bulbs. Typical of this group are *Vanda* (see p. 58), *Phalaenopsis* (see p. 56) and *Paphiopedilum* (see p. 54).

In sympodial growth, the main axis is not upright but prostrate. New shoots grow laterally from the base of the previous year's shoot (as in *Iris* species) and will eventually grow over the edge of the pot. Sympodial orchids form pseudo-bulbs and the flowers appear at the ends or along the sides. Typical examples are *Cattleya* (see p. 42) and *Cymbidium* (see p. 44).

Dendrobium primulinum from South-east Asia has strongly scented flowers that are about 6 cm (over 2 in) long.

Pseudo-bulbs

Many sympodial orchids produce conspicuous, peculiarly shaped lumps from which the leaves grow. These are thickened shoots which serve as storage organs for water and nutrients, hence the name pseudo-bulbs (see illustration p. 8) or simply bulbs (from Latin: *bulbus* = bulb). Their function is to help the orchid to survive periods of drought. These bulbs come in many different shapes: cylindrical, spindle-shaped, egg-shaped, spherical, barrel-shaped and flattened. All the pseudo-bulbs of an orchid are connected to each other by a main axis. Every year, a new, fat, smooth bulb develops and produces leaves. The old bulb becomes wrinkled and loses its leaves but continues to supply the younger bulb with nourishment.

Terrestrial and aerial roots

As in all plants, the roots of orchids are responsible for the supply and transport of water and nutrients. This is not their only purpose, however. Species that live on trees or on steep rock faces also use their roots for holding on. In this way they are able to anchor themselves so securely that it is very difficult to remove them. ***Terrestrial roots*** are found on terrestrial orchids. In tropical species these roots are generally thick, but they are thinner in European species, generally do not branch out and are often quite hairy.

The structure of a shoot
Orchids grow monopodially (left) or sympodially (right). Monopodial growth is distinguishable by the non-branching vertical shoot, from which leaves and flowers grow laterally. Sympodial orchids have a horizontal axis and pseudo-bulbs.

Aerial roots are found on epiphytic and lithophytic orchids. These roots are thick and fleshy. They are firmly rooted in soil, grip tightly to a base or dangle free in the air. Aerial roots look a lot like worms, snakes or ribbons, contain chlorophyll and are able to aid the orchid's leaves in the process of photosynthesis. A special feature of these roots is their silvery skin, called velamen. This skin consists of empty, air-filled cells which suck up and store moisture and nutrients, It also functions as insulation against ultra-violet radiation and drying heat.

Orchid leaves

Even more than the flowers, it is a study of the leaves and pseudo-bulbs which supplies information on the care a particular orchid requires (see light requirement, p. 19). In addition, you can tell by the leaves that orchids belong to the monocotyledon group of plants. Like palms, grasses and lilies, nearly all orchids possess smooth-edged leaves with veins running parallel. Divided leaves or leaves

with web-like veins are very rare. Orchid leaves may be minute or more than a metre (3 ft) across, and shaped like scales or tubes. There are broad leaves and very narrow ones, paper-thin ones and fleshy, thick ones, hard and soft ones. In some orchid species the leaves last for many years, in others they fall after one growing season.
The colour of the leaves provides information on where the plant originates. Dark green leaves generally indicate a position with poor light; fresh green leaves a position with normal lighting; grey green ones a position with an abundance of light. Many orchids possess striped leaves or leaves with a checkered pattern – some even have leaves that look like brown or green velvet shot with silver or gold threads. In these species, the flower will be small and inconspicuous, unlike the majority of orchids, in which the flower is the most spectacular part of the whole plant.

The orchid flower

Orchid flowers appear in a confusing multitude of shapes, colours, patterns, structures and scents (see p. 9). One can find flowers that are no larger than pinheads and others that extend to a metre or more across (over 3 ft) if you include the length of petals that grow into long points. Some species form single flowers, others form inflorescences with two to countless flowers, while others, again, produce thick racemes or upright spikes. The range of colours is enormous; only blue is fairly rare. Very often, individual petals appear in different colours or decorated with spots, stripes or a marbled effect.

Scented orchids
A number of orchids have developed the production of scent to a fine art in order to tempt pollinating insects. Astonishingly, some orchids are even able to change their scent depending on the customers they hope to attract at different times of the day. For example, *Phalaenopsis* smells of lily-of-the-valley during the daytime and of roses during the night. One *Dendrobium* species disperses the vanilla-like scent of heliotrope early in the morning and the scent of lilac during night-time hours. Other orchids imitate the scent of gardenias, hyacinths, stocks, primroses or jasmine. Some of the real masters among the fragrant orchids manage to produce the scent of spices, honey, fruits or leather.

Pseudo-bulbs – storage organs that come in many forms
1 Cylindrical and spindle-shaped pseudo-bulbs; 2 egg-shaped and spherical pseudo-bulbs; 3 ellipsoid pseudo-bulbs that appear flattened from the back; 4 laterally flattened pseudo-bulbs.

For example, *Odontoglossum cirrhosum*, *Oontoglossum pendulum*, *Cattleya citrina* and *Epidendrum fragrans* smell of lemons. The scent of pineapple can be found in *Aerangis crispum*. *Vandopsis* smells of leather; *Maxillaria picta* of honey. *Lycaste aromatica* and *Epidendrum radicans* carry the scent of spicy cinnamon, *Odontoglossum ornithorhynchum* and *Angraecum fragrans* smell of vanilla, while *Oncidium lanceanum* smells of cloves.

Of course, orchids do not produce their scent in order to please us but to attract pollinating insects, so there are also species which smell of mothballs or rotting meat!

The structure of the flower

In appearance an orchid flower appears complicated and yet it is sophisticatedly simple. Most orchid flowers consist of six, coloured petals arranged symmetrically on two sides. The flower consists of:

● three outer sepals (which have grown together in some species)

● two inner petals

● a conspicuously shaped and coloured lip (labellum) which is really a third, metamorphosed petal. The labellum is generally shaped like a small pouch or shoe in flowers with two fertile stamens, for example in lady's slipper orchids: in flowers with one fertile stamen it is shaped like a funnel or pipe, or is even flat with three lobes.

● the columna, a finger-like structure in the centre of the flower, which bears male and female parts. By contrast with other flowering plants in which the stamens and stigma are distinctly separate, these have usually fused in orchids. The anther, with its male pollen grains, is usually placed at the top of the tip of the columna, and the surface of the female stigma is on the underside of the front of the columna.

Pollination and seed formation

The colour, scent and structure of the flower serve purely to ensure the propagation of the species. Orchids are mainly pollinated by insects – a very few by snails, bats or hummingbirds. Every flower is not only perfectly adapted to its particular pollinator, it is also constructed in such a way that auto-pollination and self-pollination are avoided.

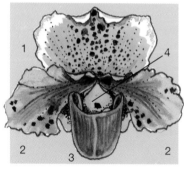

The structure of an orchid flower
All orchid flowers comprise the same parts: sepals or outer petals (1), petals (inner) (2), the lip (3) and the column (4).

Very often the flower lip bears a deceptive resemblance to the female partner of a pollinating insect and will also smell the same. After successful pollination, the petals wither and the ovary begins to swell, then ripens and forms a seed capsule. The capsule contains thousands of powder-like seeds, the very smallest and lightest of all flowering plants. Two or three seeds weigh about a millionth of a gram. In *Anguola ruckeri* up to three and a half million seeds are contained in a capsule the size of a walnut! As soon as the seed is fully ripe – which often takes months – the capsule splits open along its seams.

Flower-producing shoots

Flower-producing shoots appear on various different parts of the plant, depending on the species. In *Paphiopedilum* they emerge from the centre of the leaves which are themselves divided in two parts and grow one inside the other. In *Vanda* and *Phalaenopsis* the flowers form along the sides of the stem at an angle of about 90 degrees to the leaves. In *Dendrobium* they appear on the upperpart of the plant. In *Cattleya* and *Laelia* the flower emerges from the tip of the bulb, and in *Oncidium*, *Odontoglossum*, *Coelogyne* and *Miltonia* it appears laterally from the base of the bulb.

Are there any toxic orchids?

Orchids are not listed in most standard works on toxic plants. However, this does not mean that orchids do not produce any toxins at all as this subject has not yet been fully investigated scientifically. For this reason, we recommend that you take great care that children and domestic pets cannot gain access to your orchids. Some orchid scents can cause headaches in sensitive individuals. If you know that you react adversely to scents, you should never keep highly scented orchids in a bedroom. There have also been cases of skin infection caused by contact with the very hairy leaves of *Cypripedium pubescens*. Make sure that you wear gloves every time you handle hairy orchids.

The names of orchids

While many European orchids have both scientific and common names, most tropical species have only a proper botanical name.

Wild tropical orchids

Their names are formed from:
- the genus name, for example *Paphiopedilum*
- the species name which points out certain features, for example *callosum* = with calluses, *niveum* = snow-white, *bellatulum* = dainty, etc.
- the name of the first person to describe the species, for example Rchb. f. = Reichenbach filius
- any relevant additional information, such as a subspecies, for example *Cattleya bicolor minasgeraisensis*, or variety (var.), for example, *Paphiopedilum primulinum* var. *purpurescens*.

The common name for *Paphiopedilum* orchids is lady's slipper orchids.

Cultivated orchids

These have a similarly complicated nomenclature.

Hybrids are crosses between two species of the same genus, for example *Cymbidium ballianum*, which was created by gardeners from *Cymbidium eburneum* and *Cymbidium mastersii*. If such crosses occur in the wild, the name of this natural hybrid is written as follows: *Cymbidium x ballianum*. The term "generic hybrid" is given to the products of crosses between species and hybrids of different genera. The name is then compiled from the names of the plants concerned, for example: x *Schombocattleya* for a cross between the genus *Cattleya* and the genus *Schomburgkia*.

Multigeneric hybrids arose through crossing three or more genera, for example x *Schombolaelicattleya* from crossing *Schomburgkia*, *Laelia* and *Cattleya*. If even more orchids are involved, a new name is generally created in order to avoid unmanageably long names, for example *Potinara* (from

Coelogyne cristata loves a cool, fresh environment.

crossing *Brassavola, Laelia, Cattleya* and *Sophronitis*) or *Vuylstekeara* (from crossing *Odontoglossum, Cochlioda* and *Miltonia*).

Generic and multigeneric hybrids have a second part to their names which tells you which species of the genus were crossed. For example, *Laeliocattleya* Sheila + *Cattleya percivaliana* x *Laelia pumila*. Sheila is the grex name of the hybrid (from Latin *grex* = herd).

A "variety" is the term given to selected examples of pure species or hybrids which are propagated vegetatively (see p. 36). The variety is characterized by a third part of the plant's name, for example *Odontioda* Debutante "Oxbow".

The history of orchids

The name orchid derives from the Greek word for testicles = *orchis*. In his work *Investigations of Plants,* Theophrastus (370-285 BC) used the term to describe a group of plants with testicle-like roots, which are today known as *Orchidaceae*. This ancient text thus became the source of the name of an entire family of plants.

Exotic wonders in Europe

The innocent *Cattleya* on your windowsill – or, to be exact, its great-great grandmother – once caused one of the worst bouts of plant-hunting fever there ever was. It all began quite harmlessly. Early in the nineteenth century, a certain William Swanson shipped a cargo of tropical plants from Brazil, which he had wrapped in other tropical plants with thick stems and masses of leaves. Some of these packages found their way to a passionate plant enthusiast called Cattley. Out of sheer curiosity, Cattley took some of the plants that had been used as packaging material into his greenhouse and was amazed when they produced their first flowers in November 1818. The pink-flowering orchid with a conspicuously coloured labellum became a sensation. Dr John Lindley (1795-1865), the "father of orchid cultivation", named it *Cattleya* in honour of Mr Cattley and, on account of its attractive labellum, gave it the full name of *Cattleya labiata*. No other plant brought back from anywhere by travellers or missionaries had ever created such a fuss, not even *Bletia verrecunda* from the Bahamas, the first tropical orchid to flower in Europe in 1733! A short while later, every member of British high society appeared to be competing to see who could amass the largest collection containing the most beautiful and rare species of orchids. Money was no object and orchid mania was to cause some strange happenings. The sixth Duke of Devonshire, William George Spencer Cavendish, built a greenhouse that was 18 m (59 ft) high and 91 m (299 ft) long to house his collection of orchids, which was the largest in the world at that time.

The hunt for orchids

The demand for orchids grew to such an extent that a breed of professional orchid hunters was created. These adventurous men would often risk their lives to earn the huge sums of money that were on offer. In their quest they had to cope with tropical diseases, swarms of insects, venomous snakes, giant spiders, wild animals, hostile tribesmen and floods. In addition, they had to contend with competition from other hunters, corruption, intrigue, spying and probably murder, too. Whoever managed to survive these perils and bring the plants back safely to Europe soon became rich and also honoured, as the orchids were often named after the finder. Most imported specimens were auctioned off in London for amounts that would easily purchase a small family home nowadays. Very soon, gardeners and botanists began experimenting with these new plants.

Exclusive cultivars

In 1856, the first orchid hybrid, created from *Calanthe masuca* and *Calanthe furcata*, began to flower. In 1889 the first *Cymbidium* hybrid appeared at the Veitch nursery in England and there, in 1892, the first multigeneric hybrid was created from *Cattleya, Laelia* and *Sophronitis*. During this period, orchids also became popular as cut flowers, although they were still expensive, luxury items. At one exhibition in Germany, fifteen varieties of *Cattleya trianae* fetched between 6,000 and 10,000 DM (incredible prices) and in England the variety "Imperator" was sold for 6,000 guineas! In 1905, a trading company named Sander offered a fee of 1,000 pounds sterling to anyone who could procure a specimen of *Paphiopedilum fairrieanum*, while the highest price ever paid is reputed to have been for a specimen of *Odontoglossum crispum*.

Not until propagation from seed was finally accomplished did this madness gradually subside. Now even ordinary mortals could afford to buy them. Nowadays, they hardly cost any more than other indoor plants but they have, however, still not quite lost that aura of exclusivity, exoticism and luxury.

Purchasing orchids and finding the right position

The type of orchid you should purchase will largely be determined by the kind of position you are able to offer it. Everything else is a matter of personal preference for the colours and shapes of the flowers. Of course, cost may also play a part in your choice. If you are dealing with orchids for the very first time, it is advisable not to reach for the stars right away, i.e. the very expensive rarities – but to start with tried and tested varieties.

Where to buy orchids

Like all other special and exclusive things, you should buy your orchids in a good flower shop, in a reputable nursery or, best of all, in a plant nursery that specializes in orchids. Advice from knowledgeable employees is invaluable and essential when buying orchids which can be costly if they are rare. Furthermore, an orchid expert is in the position to put together a selection of plants tailored to your requirements, which will save you later disappointments. If you go to the trouble of making an appointment, they will probably even help you with repotting older specimens.

Orchids by post

Nearly all orchid nurseries are geared to mail order sales. Some produce catalogues containing beautiful pictures, which you can obtain for a small charge that is often refunded when you make a purchase.

Advantages for the beginner: If you are ordering orchids for the first time and are still uncertain about what to choose, you can ask the nursery to find you a suitable plant or even put together a selection. Orchids will flourish only in the right conditions, so it is important to describe to the nursery staff the position where you intend to keep your plants. They will need to know about the availability and intensity of light and you should also give them information about the average summer and winter temperatures of the site in which your orchid will live. Also, do make sure to state the colours you prefer!

Advantages for experienced orchid lovers: You can find everything in an orchid nursery, from unusual hybrids from foreign countries to attractive wild forms. There should be no problem if the nursery happens not to have the exact orchid of your choice. There are so many varieties that it is nearly always possible to find something very similar.

My tip: If you wish to purchase orchids by mail order, you must realize that nurseries will postpone sending orchids if the weather suddenly drops to below freezing or if there is a heat wave.

What to look for when purchasing orchids

Naturally, you may find yourself tempted by the glorious flowers but do not forget to check over the rest of the plant. A healthy orchid is recognizable by the following qualities:
- firm, perfect pseudo-bulbs
- numerous new shoots
- healthy, spotless foliage
- a large number of flower-bearing shoots and buds.

Further tips when purchasing

Unlike almost any other plant species, orchids are directly dependent on conditions of light and temperature. Whenever you are purchasing orchids, therefore, do make sure to check whether the variety you have chosen is suitable for the intended position.

Check the temperature range: Orchids can be assigned to three different categories of temperature and are therefore referred to as cool, temperate or warm orchids (see p. 19). Similar plants like to live together, so if you already own some orchids, choose orchids for the same position or to be in the same room from the same temperature range.

Buy well-known orchids! If no name tag is present, the names of the parent plants should at least be noted on a label. Unknown or nameless plants will present you with the difficulty of having to work out the right care.

Purchase older specimens! They are usually a bit more expensive than young plants but will also be less sensitive.

Choose plants with fully open flowers but also with some buds. They are best able to cope with transport and repositioning.

Choose hybrids instead of natural specimens! As a rule, hybrids are easier to care for and better adapted to an artificial climate and varying amounts of light.

Buy meristem-propagated plants! Meristem propagation is a special form of propagation (see p. 36). Orchids propagated in this way are cheaper as this method shortens the growing period. In addition, only healthy, well-grown parent plants that flower profusely are chosen for this method of propagation, which offers some guarantee of good health and abundant flowers.

Protection against cold when purchasing in the winter! Orchids bought in the winter should be packed up well. This is especially important for specimens in bud, which would immediately lose all their buds if subjected to the slightest touch of frost.

Spray-mist your plants instead of watering them right away! Once you have unpacked your new orchids at home, spray them with a light water mist. Leave regular watering until the next day at the earliest – and only do it then if the compost is really dry.

Holiday souvenirs and the protection of species: If you go on holiday to Thailand, the Caribbean or South America, you will be able to purchase the most splendid orchids for mere pennies. Please resist the temptation. The same goes for taking orchids from the wild – it is not only wrong, it really is not worth it! The plants you transport home will not adapt to this change as you will be unable to provide them with the conditions for acclimatizing that professional gardeners have at their disposal.

Like delicate bone china – an enlarged photograph of a Phalaenopsis.

Pink Phalaenopsis hybrid "Rudolf Baudistel" with its fiery red lip.

Most plants will not even survive the journey. In addition, you will need various official documents in order to carry plants across national borders plus a certificate to prove that the orchids are healthy, not to speak of all the formalities engendered by international plant protection regulations connected with the protection of species.

Of all flowering plants, including cacti, orchids are those most threatened with extinction. There is an absolute prohibition on the purchase of any orchids listed in Appendix 1 of the Washington Agreement on Protection of Species. One of these is *Cattleya skinneri*. My advice is always to buy orchids in a reputable nursery and to check that your supplier possesses all the documents required for trading in orchids. Many orchid nurseries sell species

Humidity for individual pots
Stand the pot on an upside-down dish in a larger, water-filled pot-holder. The inside of the bottom of the flowerpot should remain dry.

which are endangered in their countries of origin, or are even extinct in the wild. These plants will have been grown from seed or propagated by meristem.

Orchids for beginners

Orchids suitable for beginners are those natural forms and hybrids which are very adaptable and which will grow fast and flower regularly without coaxing. In general, but not always, hybrids are less sensitive than species as the raiser will have made them suitable for growing indoors.

Orchids in hydroculture

Orchids can be grown quite successfully by this method. However, you should buy your orchids in a hydroculture container from the start, as a changeover from soil to hydroculture is time-consuming and some orchids will not survive the process. Orchids grown in hydroculture should never be allowed to get "cold feet". Place a warming pad underneath the plants or insert a heating cable into the plants' container.
My tip: Use only waterproof mats and cables to avoid any accidents with electricity.
Orchids suitable for hydroculture: hybrids of *Cattleya, Phalaenopsis, Paphiopedilum, Cymbidium, Laelia* as well as *Vuylstekeara "Cambria"* and *Doritaenopsis*.
Not suitable for hydroculture: epiphytes which obtain water and fertilizers solely via their leaves, and terrestrial orchids which need to be placed in a very cool position.

Orchids for cut flowers
In florists' circles, orchids stand for luxury, although they are not as sinfully expensive as they used to be. The high price does actually justify itself as orchids usually last

much longer than other cut flowers:
● *Cymbidium* about four weeks
● *Dendrobium phalaenopsis* about three weeks
● *Paphiopedilum* and *Phalaenopsis* about two weeks
● *Cattleya, Laelia* and *Oncidium* about one week
If you wish to cut a flower from your own orchid collection then, if possible, choose specimens from the above-mentioned species or their hybrids. Among other orchids, the only suitable types are those whose flowers possess a firm, almost hard surface, are shiny or look as though they have been coated with wax. Delicate flowers with matt surfaces will not keep long when cut.

Tips on cutting
● Orchid flowers or panicles should be cut under running water.
● *Dendrobium* panicles should be briefly dipped in alcohol.
● Only use lukewarm, boiled water in vases.
● Cut the stalk again every two to three days.
● Top up any evaporated water.
● Stand the vase in a cool position at night.
● Avoid draughts.

My tip: If the flowers tend to fade too soon, slit the stem for a few centimetres and stand it, up to the flowerhead, in softened, lukewarm water for several hours.

Position and accommodation

Orchids can be kept in various ways although some species will only flourish under certain very special conditions. Possibilities include: windowsills, an open or closed picture window, a conservatory or greenhouse. Each is particularly suitable for certain types of orchids.

Windowsills

Purely from the point of view of the amount of available light, an east- or west-facing window is an ideal position for orchids (see p. 20). However, there may be a problem if a radiator is situated beneath the windowsill, as the warm, rising air may easily dry out the plants. Deft do-it-yourselfers may be able to widen the windowledge, build a protective screen for the orchids or stand a custom-built table in front of the window, which fits flush with the ledge. Raising the humidity here is essential (see p. 21).

In the case of cold, stone windowledges, insulation should be provided underneath any plants (see p. 19). The choice of orchids should depend on the conditions of light and temperature available on the relevant windowsill.

My tip: If you have french windows, stand your orchids on a shelf or stand made of glass. This will be visually pleasing and will offer the plants optimal lighting conditions.

Pot-holders
On the one hand, pot-holders hinder the circulation of air around the roots of sensitive orchids; on the other hand, the beauty of the flowers will be set off well by an attractive vessel. Take the middle path, with an air-permeable pot-holder made of basket weave, rattan or bamboo. The warm natural shades of these containers will harmonize particularly well with orchids.

Six orchids that do well on windowsills: Cattleya, Mini-Cymbidia, Odontoglossum, Oncidium, Paphiopedilum, Phalaenopsis.

Orchids in hanging containers

Plants with long, hanging flowering shoots look best grown in small wooden baskets. Grid containers are available in all sizes and can be hung in a window. This makes it

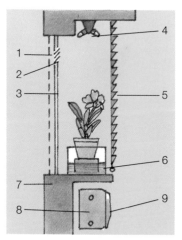

A section through an orchid window. Orchids will feel quite at home in a window set up in this way: shading (1), ventilation (2), window pane (3), plant lamp (4), inside blind (5), plant bath (6), window ledge (7), radiator (8), humidifier (9).

possible to utilize the window space for other orchids.

Six orchids which look particularly good as hanging plants: Brassavola, Coelogyne, Dendrobium, Odontoglossum, Oncidium, Phalaenopsis.

An open bay window

You are very fortunate if you already have a bay window as this will enable you to create a colony of exotic orchids. It is also possible to build such a window if you wish to do so. The built-out picture window illustrated above has a roomy plant box which has been filled with gravel or sand as a bottom layer, with a layer of peat or Hortag on top. Orchids, bromeliads or other tropical plants can be planted straight into this medium. If you wish, you can even anchor one or two epiphyte trunks in the box and tie other plants to these or hang orchid baskets or pieces of bark

with orchids in the window. This type of window will only be really successful if it is equipped with some means of shading on the outside, ventilation, an insulated window pane, additional lighting, base heating, humidity providers and room heating. All warmth-loving orchids can be kept here.

Six orchids for a built-out picture window: Dendrobium hybrids, Doritaenopsis, Doritus pulcherrima, Oncidium papilio, Paphiopedilum callosum, Phalaenopsis.

Closed picture windows and glass cases

This system creates and encloses its own micro-climate which allows the growing of the most difficult kinds of orchids. Humidity, ventilation, climate and light can all be exactly regulated by means of technology. To find out where you can obtain the equipment you need for this method of growing orchids, consult a reputable nursery. Indoor mini-greenhouses are really enclosed picture windows in miniature. If they are kept bright but not left standing in glaring sunlight, you can plant one or two orchids that require high amounts of humidity and warmth in them.

Humidity on a window ledge
Both the bath and the grid are made of plastic. Just enough water needs to be added to ensure that the orchids still have "dry feet". Check the water level in the bath frequently.

Plant suggestions for a south-facing window
(temperate to warm)
Orchids: Cymbidium, Vanda
Accompanying plants:
Allamanda, Amaryllis, Beloperone, Coleus, Crassula, Echeveria, Hibiscus

Plant suggestions for an east- or west-facing window
(temperate to warm)
Orchids: Cattleya hybrids, *Dendrobium, Laelia, Miltonia, Odontoglossum, Paphiopedilum, Phalaenopsis, Vuylstekeara*
Accompanying plants:
Aeschynanthus, Anthurium, leaf begonias, bromeliads (various), *Caladium, Codiaeum, Dieffenbachia,* ferns, *Fittonia, Philodendron* species, *Pilea, Spathiphyllum,* African violets

Plant suggestions for a north-facing window
(cool to temperate)
Orchids: Coelogyne, Dendrobium nobile, Odontonia, Oncidium, Zygopetalum
Accompanying plants:
cyclamens, *Araucaria, Azalea, Chamaedorea, Cissus antarctica, Cryptanthus, Epipremnum,* ferns, *Ficus pumila, Camellia, Rhapis, Saxifraga stolonifera, Tolmiea*

choose the temperature range. Depending on your choice of plants, you should then be able to cultivate many orchids of the same temperature range.

Orchids combined with other plants

Most orchid lovers are of the opinion that, just like at home, orchids in "exile" tend to flourish in the company of other plants. This is partly because neighbouring plants – particularly plants with many or large leaves – produce plenty of moisture through evaporation, thereby contributing to the general humidity.

Six orchids suitable for enclosed picture windows or a glass case: *Angraecum* species, *Doritis pulcherrima, Oncidium kramerianum, Paphiopedilum callosum, Phalaenopsis.*

Conservatories
Conservatories provide a wonderful opportunity for cultivating orchids as they are usually built on to the house. This makes care considerably easier than would be the case in a free-standing greenhouse. If the conservatory is heatable, temperate to warm orchids can be cultivated there; if it is cool, like a bedroom, cool to temperate plants are better suited.
Orchids for cool to temperate conservatories: Coelogyne, hybrids of *Cymbidium;* cool *Dendrobia, Disa uniflora, Masdevallia;* cool *Miltonia, Odontocidium* hybrids; *Odontoglossum (Rossioglossum) grande, Odontoglossum* hybrids; *Oncidium* hybrids; cool, green-leafed *Paphiopedilum, Vuylstekeara Cambria, Zygopetalum.*

Orchids for temperate to warm conservatories: Ascocenda hybrids; *Cattleya* hybrids; warm *Dendrobia, Dendrobium phalaenopsis, Laelia* hybrids; warm *Oncidia, Paphiopedilum* hybrids; *Phalaenopsis* hybrids; *Vanda* hybrids.

Greenhouses
Many an impassioned orchid lover, faced with an ever-growing orchid collection, has resorted to building a greenhouse for his beloved plants out in the garden. It goes without saying, however, that, even in a greenhouse, you cannot manage without the aid of special gadgets for heating, humidity regulation, light, shade and ventilation. These are the ideal positions for greenhouses:
● near the house because of necessary power and water supplies
● if possible, near a tree with foliage which will provide shade in the summer and allow light to penetrate through its branches in the winter. With the help of technology, you will be able to

Orchid societies

If you like to spend time growing and talking about orchids, I recommend joining your local or county society of orchid lovers. Most countries have at least a national orchid society. The society will be able to provide help and advice about obtaining new plants and solving problems. The publications issued by such a society bring members up to date on the latest developments in botany, raising, care and the practical side of growing orchids. Among the activities of a good society are the running of events, courses, slide shows and workshops on sowing, propagation and the culture of indigenous orchids. Study trips are also sometimes arranged. To find out the address and location of your nearest or national orchid society, enquire at your local garden centre or from the specialist orchid grower from whom you bought or intend to buy your plants. You could also write to the Royal Botanic Gardens at Kew in London.

Orchid care all year round

Orchids have a different life cycle to most other indoor plants. They do not grow in garden soil or ordinary houseplant compost, but in a special orchid compost and require relatively few nutrients. If you manage the harmonious combination of the five elements of temperature, light, air, humidity and nutrients, you will be richly rewarded with plants that live long and produce enchanting flowers.

The growth cycle

As with all plants, the life of orchids is characterized by an alternating cycle of growth periods and rest periods. If you want your plants to produce flowers every year, you must become very familiar with this natural programme as the demands and needs of orchids differ depending on the particular phase they are in.

The rest phase: The rest phase corresponds to the tropical period of drought which, in turn, approximates to the winter period of temperate zones. Many orchids flower at the beginning of, during or shortly after this rest phase. If they are kept too moist during this phase, orchids will not produce flowers and will only form weak new shoots.

General rule: Orchids with tough leaves and greatly reduced or almost absent bulbs should never be allowed to dry out completely. Exact data on individual measures of care can be found on page 39 et sec.

The right temperature

In the wild, orchids grow in the most diverse climatic zones. Some flourish in continually moist, warm regions, others in regions that are warm and moist some of the time, others again in regions that are dry and hot in the daytime and moist and cool at night. Finally, there are those orchids that love moist, cool regions. The general rule for the care of orchids is to establish where

they can be assigned in the rough division into the three temperature categories: cool, temperate or warm. It is very important to know the exact temperature requirements of individual orchids. Within one genus (for example, *Dendrobium*, see p. 46) you can find species belonging to each of the three different temperature ranges. For this reason, you should always enquire as to the correct name of a plant on purchasing (see p. 12).

The result of a temperature drop at night: In the natural habitats of orchid species that like a lot of warmth, night-time temperatures are often around 7-12°C lower than the daytime values. This night-time temperature drop is necessary for the formation of flowers in many orchids and should be at least 4-6°C (39-43°F). Basically, the following rule applies: the warmer the temperature, the higher the humidity (see p. 12).

My tip: If you want to grow several different orchids, remember to choose only those species that belong to one range of temperature for one position (see table, p. 19).

Growth and care

Time	Vegetation phase	Requirements of care
Late winter/spring	New shoots	More light, more water
Early summer/summer	Growth	Nutrients, water, warmth
Late summer/early autumn	Bulbs, ripe shoots, formation of buds	Night-time drop in temperature, plenty of light in autumn, reduce water gradually
Autumn/winter	Rest phase, flowering phase	More light, little water

How to measure the temperature

In general, the kind of temperatures we feel comfortable with indoors during the summer and winter will also suit most orchids. A simple indoor thermometer is sufficient for checking the temperature. Better still is a mini-max thermometer which records the highest and lowest temperatures so that one can easily read the differences in temperature between day and night. No matter which thermometer you decide on, place it near your plants, as the temperature near a window may differ considerably from that in the centre of a room.

Approx. temperature ranges during the annual cycle

Temperature range	Summer/ daytime	Summer/ night-time	Winter/ daytime	Winter/ night-time
cool	16°C/61°F	13°C/55°F	13°C/55°F	10°C/50°F
temperate	20°C/68°F	8°C/64°F	16°C/61°F	13°C/55°F
warm	25°C/77°F	20°C/68°F	20°C/68°F	18°C/64°F

Temperature and position

The following unfavourable conditions for orchids should be avoided if possible:
● direct sunlight; this will rapidly raise the temperature in spite of shade and humidity
● plants placed too close to the window pane; this may lead to overheating of the leaves
● cold stone window ledges; during the winter they may often be several degrees cooler than the average room temperature
● draughts near a badly insulated window.

What to watch out for in winter

Perform the "candle test" if your orchids are to be left on a windowsill during the winter. Stand a lit candle on the windowsill. If the flame remains still and upright, the

Orchids in a window
Such a bright spot is just what these plants need for optimal, healthy development. Here: Cattleya (pink) hybrids, Phalaenopsis (pink and white), Oncidium (yellow) and Paphiopedilum (violet) grow happily.

window is well insulated, but if it moves sideways or flickers, you should insulate the cracks around the window. In the case of cold stone window ledges, use an electric heating pad or at least a thick sheet of polystyrene for insulation underneath the plant pots or orchid container. Even orchids from cool regions will not cope with "cold feet". In their countries of origin, the air may be cool and fresh but the soil always remains relatively warm.
Remember also that orchids that remain on a windowsill above a radiator during the winter will require additional moisture (see p. 21).

Measuring the amount of light

Along with temperature, light influences the most important life processes: germination, growth and the formation of flowers. The light requirements of orchids tend to be determined by their temperature requirements in their natural environments.
Light requirements: Among other factors, adaptation to light has influenced the shape of orchids for millions of years. Even if you own a "nameless" plant, you can still work out its light requirements by studying certain characteristics of the plant:

● Terrestrial orchids without bulbs and with relatively soft leaves do not need direct sunlight.
Example: (*Paphiopedilum*).
● Epiphytes with large, fleshy leaves and no bulbs will not cope well with a lot of sunlight either.
Example: (*Phalaenopsis*).
● Orchids with relatively tough leaves with large surfaces and relatively well-developed bulbs will not require direct sunlight until they reach the flowering stage and begin to open.
Examples: *Cattleya, Cymbidium, Laelia, Odontoglossum, Oncidium.*
● Orchids with narrow, tough, leathery leaves and large bulbs are genuine sunlovers.
Example: *Vanda.*
● Orchids with narrow leaves, almost like stems, or with striated leaves, and with no bulbs are well adapted to great intensity of light.
Example: *Dendrobium striolatum.*

How to measure light

In general, orchids thrive in light intensities of 6,000-10,000 lux. These values are normally to be found in windows. However, remember that even only 1 m (3 ft) away from the window, the light intensity will be only a quarter of that near the window. An exact measurement of light can only be carried out with a luxmeter (obtainable from garden or photographic suppliers).

The splendid flowers of a well-cared-for miniature Cymbidium. This specimen is more than ten years old.

The best window position

Once you have made sure that the window is not open to the sky nor obscured or overshadowed by trees or other houses, the following guidelines can be accepted:

● East- and west-facing windows (3,000-5,000 lux) are the best positions.

● North-facing windows (800-1,000 lux) are really only suitable during the very light summer months and even then only for species that can cope with lots of shade.

● South-facing windows (up to 20,000 lux) are perfect during the winter. During the spring, summer and autumn, however, they will have to be provided with shade using curtains, blinds, sheets of tissue paper or with the help of neighbouring plants: during early spring between 11 a.m. and 4 p.m.; from early summer onwards between 10 a.m. and 6 p.m.

My tip: The more humid and airy the position in which an orchid is placed, the lighter and warmer it may be.

Light from the mains

Even in a north-facing window or in a dark corner of a room, orchids will thrive with artificial lighting. Do remember, however, that ordinary light bulbs will not supply the right light for plants! I recommend special plant strip lights, two of which can be installed at intervals of 6 cm (just over 2 in) about 50 cm (20 in) above the orchids. Ask a professional electrician to install these and also have a timer switch fitted so that the lamps can be turned on and off on demand.

An alternative to this form of lighting is attractive hanging or wall lamps. They can be installed individually or in rows. As these kinds of lamps will require special fixtures, you should, again, get an electrician to install them for you. One hour of additional illumination with these lamps will cost only a few pence.

Warning: Only buy lamps that are resistant to splashes with water and make sure that they carry the British Standard kitemark. All electrical installations should be carried out by a professional electrician.

Artificial light – when and for how long? The sum of natural and artificial light should not exceed 14 hours, otherwise your orchids will go on strike when it comes to flowering, just as they would if they were receiving too little light. Turn on the plant lamps:

● if you grow your orchids in a cellar, for a maximum of 14 hours per day
● on sunny autumn and winter days in the mornings and afternoons
● on dull autumn and winter days for 12 hours during the daytime.

My tip: Plant lamps give a real boost to freshly repotted orchids or those damaged by too much shade. If you own only one lamp, give the orchids a "light bath" if you are trying to coax them to flower. You can find out about the right times to do this in the section on individual care (see p. 39).

Humid air

Humidity levels of 60-70% are the ideal conditions in which orchids will feel really comfortable.
During the summer, lack of humid air is not a great problem. In fine weather the humidity levels indoors will be about 50%; during dull, rainy

weather 60-80%. Outside, in well-ventilated summer quarters, especially during thundery weather, conditions may be even better still. The critical time is during the winter, when the warmth from central heating systems eats away at the humidity levels in the air. In addition, in most homes the central heating radiators are situated right underneath windowsills. This means that the humidity level may rapidly drop to below 40% which is much too low for orchids (and even for most other indoor plants).

What is humidity?
Humidity or "relative humidity" is defined by the percentage of water vapour molecules in the air. 0% = absolutely dry, 100% = saturated water vapour mist.

How to measure humidity
A gadget called a hygrometer is used to measure humidity levels. It can be part of an entire home "weather station", together with a thermometer and a barometer, or you can buy the individual pieces of equipment. These items make it possible for orchid growers to monitor humidity levels. You can observe how these levels constantly change. If the level drops below 60%, it will become necessary to take action.

How to raise humidity levels
The best tried and tested gadgets for raising humidity levels are misters, electrical humidifiers, a plastic grid or a specially equipped plant container (see illustration, p. 22).

A mister bottle or spray attachment: These will supply sufficient humidity for everyday use. Adjust the mister outlet to its finest setting and spray only the leaves, not the flower! Just as when watering, it is better to spray the

leaves in the mornings. The plant will then have plenty of time during the day to dry off before the temperature drops again at night.
Warning: Do not spray any plants while the sun is shining on them! The minute droplets of water will act like magnifying glasses in sunlight and may cause burns on the leaves.
An electric humidifier will supply a constant rate of humidity during the central-heating season indoors. This can be obtained from electrical suppliers or orchid suppliers.
A plastic grid: All that you need is a rectangular dish and a grid insert, both made of plastic (see p. 15). This dish, which can accommodate several orchids at once, will have a constant supply of water in it so that the plants always have dry feet but will be permanently surrounded by evaporating water and thus enjoy plenty of humidity.
A plant bath (see illustrations, p. 22) is filled with Hortag or peat. This substance should be kept permanently moist so that it can release water vapour into the air.
Further tricks for increasing humidity
● Stand bowls of water between your orchid pots.
● Place dishes of permanently moist Hortag, sand or gravel under upside-down pot-holders with orchid pots standing on top of them.
● Use larger pot-holders with the spaces between the pot and pot-holder filled with Hortag or peat that is kept constantly moist. This method will only work properly with orchids in clay pots!
● Use waterfalls, indoor fountains, a spring stone surrounded with plants or aquariums.
● Supply large-leafed, neighbouring plants which evaporate plenty of water, for example *Araceae, Maranta* or bromeliads.
● Use marginal plants which stand permanently in water, like *Cyperus*.

My tip: Use distilled water for misting or spraying (obtainable in chemists, etc.). This will prevent chalky deposits on window panes. Water in evaporation dishes, which does not come into direct contact with the plants, need not be softened. If chalk deposits appear on the insides of dishes, they can be removed with diluted vinegar.

Fresh air – but no draughts!

Regular airing or ventilation is extremely important for the well-being of orchids – in particular for their aerial roots! Fresh air will prevent decay and the proliferation of fungi and pests. There are many ways to supply extra oxygen:
● by opening or tilting the window
● by installing a sliding ventilation hatch or tip-hatch
● by means of a ventilator on the inside of the window
● by means of electrical ventilation
● by allowing the plant to live outside during the summer months.

My tip: If you air the room in the winter, you should cover up the plants beforehand or move them from the windowsill. Cold draughts are lethal for them.

Avoid the scent of apples!

In contrast to bromeliads, whose flowering is triggered by the odour of apples, orchids react with falling buds or flowers. The cause is the ethylene gas released by apples, so never stand a fruit bowl close to your orchids!

Correct watering

Orchids love contact with water but this experience should be brief. In particular, the compost must dry off rapidly afterwards. Not for nothing do orchids thrive on permeable, porous planting substances which allow water to drain away quickly as through a coarse sieve. This alternating of wetness and dryness will make them feel right at home, as will the alternating daily rhythm of heat and night-time coolness. Waterlogging will kill off any orchid!

The best water for watering
Water should always be at room temperature, slightly acid and soft. With the exception of some lady's slipper species, all orchids hate lime. Rainwater or melted snow in the winter is usually soft, but with increasing atmospheric pollution these days they are rapidly losing

their good qualities in many areas.
My tip: Collect rainwater, allow it to run through a paper coffee filter and then allow it to stand for a few days. You can also purify rainwater using household water filters.
If you use mains water for watering, you should check the acidity content (pH value) and the hardness of the water.
The acidity content is easy to measure with a strip of indicator paper (obtainable from chemists or aquarium suppliers). The values are expressed in degrees of pH. The scale extends from 1-14, and the neutral reading is in the middle at 7; all figures below 7 are in the acid range; all figures above 7 are in the alkaline range. Orchids prefer weakly acid water with a pH value of around 5 or 6.
The hardness of the water can be ascertained by enquiring at your local water authority.
It is measured in degrees Clark:
  0-10 = soft water
 11-20 = medium hard water
 21-38 = hard water
Orchids can tolerate water with a hardness degree of, at most, 13 degrees Clark, although a very few can cope with values up to 15 degrees Clark. If your mains water value is above this, you will have to soften it.
How to soften water: In the case of medium hard to soft water, a few drops of lemon juice will be sufficient to soften it.
Harder water has to be properly treated. (All preparations and gadgets are obtainable in the gardening trade.)
● With water-softening agents in tablet, powder or liquid form. These will precipitate lime and other undesirable substances from the water. If you decant the water carefully after several hours, the lime deposits will settle at the bottom of the container.

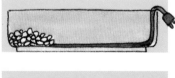

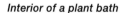
Interior of a plant bath

Lay a plastic heating cable in a flowerbox without drainage holes. Fix it in position with a little gravel. Place upside-down flowerpots in the box. Sprinkle Hortag, sand, gravel or peat between them and add water to 1 cm (under ½ in) beneath the base of the pots. Stand pots of orchids on top.

● Ion exchange fertilizers are able to exchange substances that produce hardness for those that produce softness.
● Using a watering can with a filter attachment containing ion exchangers that get rid of lime and chlorine.
● Fill a small linen sack with peat and suspend it in a bucket of water.
● Boil the water. This will remove limescale. Unfortunately, it will also get rid of most of the oxygen.

Immersing instead of watering
Orchids in hanging baskets are not easy to water as the water tends to run out. Immersing the entire container in water will do the trick just as well. Hang the basket up again as soon as the water has drained out.

My tip: Whatever type of mains water you have, it may contain chlorine which orchids have difficulty in coping with. To be safe, allow the water to stand overnight before using it. Using water from water-softening gadgets can also be risky as salts that can be harmful to orchids may be present.

How often to water
This will depend on many individual factors:
● on the type of growing medium, which will absorb more or less water depending on its consistency
● on the plant container being used; orchids in plastic pots will not dry out as fast as those in clay pots. Plants in airy hanging baskets or growing on branches will dry out quickest
● on the humidity level; the higher this is, the less often you need to water
● on the temperature; the warmer and sunnier the weather, the quicker water will evaporate
● air movement; windy conditions in the plants' summer quarters or a ventilator in a window will cause the growing medium to dry out faster
● on the growth of the plants; an orchid that is going through a growth phase and is producing many new shoots will require more water than a plant that has finished growing and is conserving energy for the ripening of its bulbs and for forming flowers. If you give too much water now, the orchid will produce masses of leaves instead of flowers.

The finger test: Push a finger fairly deep into the growing medium. If it feels dry, give the orchid a vigorous watering. Allow the pot to drain off well afterwards. The growing medium should not be allowed to become too dry or it will have difficulty absorbing water. If the medium feels moist and slightly cool, do not water.

Watering during vacations

How to water
Orchids are best watered from above so that the growing medium is moistened all through. Do not allow water to run over the plant itself. Orchids that are tied to branches or installed in hanging baskets can be dunked in a bucket of water several times (see illustration, left).

My tip: Watering and spraying are best done in the mornings. This will allow the plant enough time to dry off before the inevitable slight drop in temperature towards evening or when the heating is turned down for the night. This method will prevent a harmful drop in temperature due to evaporation in the root area.

Watering during absences
All irrigation systems currently on the market work on the principle of capillary action. Water conductors are inserted into the compost or planting medium, in the shape of cones, wicks, felt discs, mats or absorbent wood. These constantly absorb water from a reservoir to which they are connected. The larger the reservoir of water, the longer the plants can be left to their own devices. However, this system is not entirely problem-free with such sensitive plants as orchids.

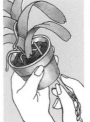

Using a heavy-duty needle, draw an absorbent wick up through the drainage hole at the base of the pot and through the compost. Thread the wick through a drinking straw, then arrange it on the surface of the compost and cover it with a thin layer of compost. If the plant has a compact root system, remove it from its pot beforehand. If the lower half of the compost is coarse and well-aired, this method will function even better.

I have experienced satisfying results with such systems (see illustration, p. 23). The inventor of this method keeps thousands of orchids and yet is able to go off on holiday for three weeks at a time.

Mistakes in watering

Unfortunately, mistakes in care do not always become immediately obvious. Often it is already too late to put things right once they are noticed. You may have either watered too often or too much if:
● the leaves go limp, drop off or turn yellow
● the roots are decaying
● growth ceases.

You have given too little water if:
● the pseudo-bulbs shrivel
● the roots turn brown and wither
● the leaves go limp, drop off or turn yellow.

Watering orchids in their summer quarters

In conditions of constant high pressure, orchids will rapidly dry out and may have to be watered daily. During periods of damp weather, on the other hand, the growing medium may stay wet for too long. If there is continuous rainfall for longer than two days and there is no prospect of an improvement in the weather, it is preferable to place the orchids beneath an overhanging roof or something similar. Orchids hanging in tree branches can be placed on a patio wall that is shaded from direct sunlight. It is very important never to place orchid pots directly on the ground or on a table as it is absolutely essential that air is able to circulate beneath the pot and that even the slightest bit of waterlogging is avoided. In the case of large containers, place a few bricks underneath them, and place small pots on a lattice-top table or on a grid.

Spring-flowering Lycaste fimbriata should be kept in temperate to cool surroundings.

Fertilizing

Basically, orchids are small eaters. However, bearing in mind that a plant container limits their living space, they do need to be supplied with nutrients from an outside source, which means that they need fertilizing. This is especially true for modern hybrids which are raised for vigorous growth and the formation of plenty of flowers. In addition, these days more and more synthetic components are added to the planting mediums used for orchids. Unlike fern roots or bark, these substances do not gradually decompose and, therefore, do not release any nutrients.

The right fertilizer

In principle, the orchid could not care less whether the supply of nutrients it is offered is bound organically or minerally. The main thing is that nutrients are supplied at the right moment and this is simplest with the use of water-soluble, mineral fertilizers in which the nutrients are instantly available for the use of the orchid. Organic fertilizers, on the other hand, require the presence of active micro-organisms in the soil around the roots, will only break down slowly and are not instantly available to the plant. If you use organic fertilizers, you will need to know all about the growth cycle of your plants and this is not always a simple matter in the case of orchids.

The simplest method for beginners is to use the orchid fertilizers that are sold in the gardening trade, at specialist orchid nurseries or through mail order firms dealing with orchids. Do not use fertilizer intended for vegetables etc.

Huntleya meleagris has similar requirements to Phalaenopsis.

Follow the dosage recommended on the packet. If you really have to, you can use ordinary flower fertilizers but these need to be diluted ten times for orchids, otherwise the roots will be burnt. I recommend counting out the recommended dosage of such liquid fertilizer using an eye-dropper, dividing the amount by ten and allowing the resulting dose to dribble into 1 litre (1¾ pt) of water. In the case of powdered fertilizer, again use only one tenth of the recommended dose in 1 litre of water.

When and how to fertilize

This is hard to determine exactly. Frequency of fertilization will depend on the size, age and individual growth of the orchid and also on the species, and may vary quite considerably. Detailed information is given in the section on individual care (see p. 39).
In general:
● Fertilize every four days from late spring to late summer, or fertilize along with every third watering.
● Fertilize once a week from late winter to mid-spring and during early and mid-autumn.
● Do not fertilize at all during late autumn to late winter.

Five rules to follow:

● Fertilize more often using a greatly diluted fertilizer, rather than seldom with a more concentrated dose.
● Only fertilize while the plants are growing and require nutrients for their development – never during their rest period.
● Never pour fertilizer on to a dry growing medium.
● Only fertilize well-rooted, healthy plants.

● Never fertilize freshly repotted plants.
My tip: Orchids may also be fertilized via their leaves. Leaf fertilizing involves spraying a fine mist of diluted fertilizer all over the leaves. This is particularly recommended for orchids with sick or meagre roots. Leaf fertilizing also protects the growing medium from becoming clogged with salts.

Repotting

Really experienced orchid growers like to prepare their own growing medium according to their own recipe. If you have only a few plants on your windowsill, however, you are better off purchasing a commercially produced standard orchid compost. Ask a reputable orchid grower what medium to use for individual species of orchids.
My tip: When purchasing or ordering orchids, obtain one or two bags of orchid-growing medium at the same time, so that you have it handy.

Important points

Whether you buy ready-made compost or mix your own, every orchid-growing medium should have the following characteristics:
● It should be air- and water-permeable and retain warmth.
● It should be lightweight and loose but still hold the plant securely.
● It should absorb water easily but also drain quickly.
● Nutrients should not break down too quickly so that there is a flood of nutrients all at the same time, thereby raising the salts content in the medium.
● It should show a slightly acid pH value (see p. 22).
Warning: Do not use ordinary, undiluted flower compost for orchids! It is totally unsuitable.

Tying up a tall plant
Tall-growing orchids will require support after repotting and can be tied to a stick made of bamboo or wood. Secure the shoots with loose, figure-of-eight-shaped loops of twine, soft plant wire or anchoring clips.

The constituents of orchid-growing mediums

Orchids may be grown in organic, mineral or synthetic mediums or in a mixture of all three.
The classic orchid-growing mediums contain fern roots, tree ferns (like *Xaxim* and *Mexifern*) and *Sphagnum* moss. All three can still be obtained from orchid suppliers but no one knows for how much longer this will be possible as regulations designed for the protection of species and various nature protection agreements prohibit any future plundering of these natural resources.
Modern orchid-growing mediums consist of:
● peat products, such as moss peat, sedge peat, peat compost
● types of tree bark, like *Meranti*, redwood, cork oak, pine bark and cork chips

● polystyrene products like orchid chips (see p. 27) or polystyrene flakes
● charcoal
● mineral substances, like Hortag (for orchids in hydroculture), pumice gravel, glimmer, shell lime, dolomite lime, lava and perlite.
This group also includes chippings of a mineral-rich volcanic stone whose weight will provide anchorage even for tall-growing orchids. Although the pH value of this substance (at 7.5) is rather high, orchids appear to thrive on it. Particularly good results have been obtained with *Odontoglossum grande* (see p. 50).

What these substances do
Mineral constituents provide minerals and trace elements.
Synthetic substances prevent rapid clogging, waterlogging or rapid cooling down of the planting medium. They also promote better ventilation.
Natural or organic substances support root formation and provide nutrients. Charcoal chunks prevent infections and decay. In the case of terrestrial orchids, a little standard compost is often added as a source of nutrients or a little loam may be

added to give the medium "hold".
Warning: The pine needles or beech leaves that are often used in growing mediums for orchids can be carriers of disease!

Good mediums for orchids
Add a specialist orchid fertilizer to your own growing medium mixtures. Make sure that you follow the dosage instructions to the letter. Specialist fertilizer contains all the important trace elements for a good start in the new vegetation cycle. Do not use ordinary fertilizers.

For epiphytes in pots
● Recipe 1
1 part cork chips
1 part pine bark
1 part polystyrene flakes
½ part peat
½ part charcoal
2 g carbonic acid powder per litre growing medium

● Recipe 2
5 parts fine pine bark
2 parts peat
2 parts pumice gravel
1 part charcoal
2 g carbonic acid powder per litre growing medium

Repotting

First fill a third of the new pot with coarse polystyrene flakes. Add a handful of fresh compost. Stand the plant on top. Surround the rootstock with additional compost. Press down. Leave an edge of 1-2 cm (½-¾ in) for watering. Sympodial orchids like Cattleya (see above) should be placed in such a way that the new shoot is pointing towards the centre of the pot. Monopodials should be set right in the centre.

For terrestrial orchids
2 parts pine bark
1 part peat
1 part fine compost
a little loam

My tip: Never throw away packaging material made of polystyrene. If it is chopped up small, this can be reused by adding it to compost or as a layer for drainage purposes.

Orchids in polystyrene

The most modern types of compost are completely synthetic. Orchid chips are made from a polystyrene mixture with a very rough surface. These chips have proved very successful in practical trials with all orchids which can be grown in this medium alone.
Important: If you are growing your plants in orchid chips, you should fertilize them all year round.

Plant containers

Whether you grow your orchids in pots or wooden containers will depend largely on your own taste and on the position of the plants. A flowerpot is still the best type of container for a windowsill. If you have a plant window with a climate specially adapted to plants, you may place your plants in decorative hanging containers or tie them to pieces of bark, branches or roots.

Selecting pots
Nowadays most orchids are offered for sale in plastic or clay pots.
Clay pots are air- and water-permeable and are more stable because of their weight, but they dry out a lot faster than plastic pots and may allow salts to accumulate which, in turn, can burn the roots of orchids under certain conditions. In addition, these pots may look

The right way to secure orchids to a base
Place plant compost in front of and behind the roots. Tie the plant to the tree fern block or piece of bark in such a way that no water is able to run into the heart of the plant. Tie up the plant with strips of ladies' tights.

unsightly after some time, due to deposits of lime on their sides.
Plastic pots do not allow the compost to dry out so quickly and will always remain clean but they do tip over rather easily. The best plastic pots have thick walls in light colours, which do not break so easily and will not heat up quite so much in strong sunlight.
Containers or large plant tubs made of terracotta, wood, ceramic or plastic make ideal plant containers for large, spreading orchids like *Cymbidia*.

Lattice baskets
These are very suitable for orchids with flowers that hang down (see p. 15). Lattice baskets have the advantage of allowing air to reach the compost and roots all round. As they may look dry from the outside but still be moist on the inside, you will need to be careful about watering them (see illustration, p. 23).

Pieces of bark, branches and roots
The orchid and its compost material are tied to this growing base (see p. 28 and illustrations above). The most suitable materials are cork or the bark of pine or oak.
My tip: Special expandable planting boxes can be used for smaller,

sympodially growing orchids. These can be expanded when required, which avoids the necessity to repot the plant.

The right way to repot

Any kind of repotting is stressful to orchids. Repotting will, however, become necessary in the following circumstances:
● If the compost has become hard and dense and is no longer air- or water-permeable.
● If the plant is too large for the pot and is constantly in danger of tipping over.
● If a plant's new growth is becoming too much for the old pot and is beginning to grow over the edge.
● If the plant is sick (see p. 30).

How often should a plant be repotted?
The frequency of repotting will depend a great deal on the shape of growth of the orchid and also on the type of compost. Plants may grow happily for years in completely synthetic polystyrene chips for example. Natural compost material, which will decompose and break down over a period of time, will have to be renewed more often.

Sympodially growing orchids will have to be repotted approximately every two to three years on average, for example *Cattleya* (see illustration, p. 8), *Cymbidium, Laelia, Odontoglossum, Oncidium*. **Monopodial** orchids are, as a rule, repotted every three to four years, for example *Vanda. Paphiopedilum* and *Phalaenopsis* (see illustration, p. 8) should, however, be repotted every two to three years.

When to repot

Always repot at the beginning of a new growth period. You will recognize that the time is right by the appearance of fresh, light green shoots and when the orchid begins to form new roots. In many species, the ideal time lies between late winter and late spring. Some orchid growers like to repot after flowering is over. Some consider late summer – particularly for *Phalaenopsis* – the most favourable time.

My tip: Do not wait too long before replanting an orchid in a new pot. By the time the plant has finger-length new shoots it will find the change harder to cope with.

Preparing the new pot

The new container should be absolutely clean and not too large because a very thick layer of compost in a pot that is too large tends to prevent oxygen from reaching the roots. Remember to soak clay pots in water for 24 hours before repotting.

Ensure that an adequate drainage layer is placed at the bottom of a new pot. The layer should be 1-3 cm (up to 1¼ in) thick and consist of polystyrene flakes, pumice gravel, Hortag or clay pot shards (see illustration, p. 26).

How to repot

The main requirements are gentle hands and lots of patience. Above

all things, an orchid will not take kindly to damaged roots.

Step 1: Water the plant well the day before repotting so that its roots are smooth and flexible rather than dry and brittle.

Step 2: Carefully loosen the rootstock in the old pot. If it is stuck, cut a plastic pot open along the side or break a clay pot with a hammer. Orchids in wooden containers should have their roots carefully loosened before removing them.

Step 3: Now shake the rootstock gently without allowing the plant to fall apart. Parts of the roots that look diseased, dried up or shrunken should be cut off with a very sharp knife or with scissors. Plants that are too large or very old can be divided when repotting and thereby rejuvenated (see p. 36).

My tip: To avoid the risk of infection, first disinfect your knife or scissors with alcohol and then treat the cut surface of the plant with charcoal powder.

Step 4: Place a thin layer of new compost on top of the drainage layer in the prepared pot. Place the rootstock on top of this and surround it with the rest of the compost. While doing this, occasionally tap the pot against the edge of the table to help the compost particles to shake down into all the cracks and spaces. This gets rid of hollow spaces between the roots and will help the roots to make thorough contact with the compost.

Note: Monopodial orchids (like *Paphiopedilum* or *Phalaenopsis*) should be placed in the centre of the pot.

Sympodial orchids (like *Cattleya, Dendrobium* or *Laelia*) can be potted in such a way that the oldest bulb is close to the edge of the pot while the new shoot is in the centre. This is the only way that the plant

can spread unhindered. Aerial roots which have developed facing towards the compost can be packed with compost as this will help the plant to gain a firmer hold. They can also be allowed to hang over the edge of the pot.

Step 5: Allow a space of 1-2 cm (up to ¾ in) around the plant for watering purposes.

My tip: Very tall or heavy plants with relatively weak roots may sometimes have a tendency to tip over after repotting in loose, soft compost. The best plan is to drive a stick made of wood, bamboo or plastic deep into the compost and tie the plant to it to give it support as it grows (see illustration, p. 26).

After repotting

● Place the freshly repotted plant in a bright, but on no account sunny, position.

● New root formation will be encouraged if a heating mat is placed underneath the pots.

● In contrast to most indoor plants, orchids should not be given water immediately after repotting. This is because the damaged parts of roots are better able to heal in compost that is merely moist and fresh from the bag. Also, a minimum of moisture encourages the roots to grow in order to seek it (see increasing humidity, p. 21).

● After eight to 14 days, the plant may be watered normally and according to its requirements.

● Orchids tied to a base (see illustration, p. 27) should also be placed in a bright but not too sunny position. During the first two weeks, spray but do not water.

Sought-after cut flowers

Cymbidia are among the most popular orchids for florists. Green or green yellow hybrids, like this "Vanguard", are particularly unusual.

Mistakes in care, pests and diseases

Orchids are really quite tough and resilient but they are not immune to attack by insects, fungi, viruses or bacteria. In addition, mistakes in care may make them sick and unsightly. Optimal care is always the best preventive measure.

Taking preventive measures

The best way to ensure the good health of your orchids is to learn about the requirements of each particular species and make sure that you make good hygiene your normal practice.
● If you have to turn up the heating, make sure that you also increase humidity. This will prevent attack by insects.
● Remove all decaying, dried up or yellow leaves.
● Always replace compost that shows a layer of white fungus.
● Place affected plants in quarantine immediately so that they will not infect others.
● All knives and other cutting tools should be disinfected with pure alcohol.
● Cut surfaces of plants, or injuries, should be disinfected with charcoal powder.
● Plant containers that are to be reused should be scrubbed in a hot soapy solution and rinsed thoroughly in clear water afterwards.

Methods of control

Chemical: sprays or watering with insecticides and fungicides.
Mechanical: removing infested or diseased parts of plants and collecting pests by hand.
Biological: employing natural predators like predatory mites and other useful insects (see p. 34).
Alternatives: use herbal infusions, plastic bags or natural plant protection sprays which are now being used with considerable success in professional nurseries. For suggestions and recipes, see page 34.
My tip: The manufacturers' instructions should be strictly followed when using any plant protection agents. Orchids will react sensitively to high dosages. When using plant sprays, do so from a sufficient distance so that the plants do not suffer from "cold burns" caused by the propellant. Plant sprays without a propellant or with a harmless propellant are more environmentally friendly.

Mistakes in care

Problems nearly always arise because of mistakes in care.

Crippled growth; cessation of growth
Symptoms: bad smell, algal growth, decaying roots.
Cause: a position that is too dark; more rarely lack of nutrients.
Remedy: repot the plant, cut off decayed roots, disinfect the plant or repot it in fresh compost.

Sunburn
Symptoms: at first yellowish-white, later brownish, spots on the uppersides of leaves.
Causes: Plants too close to the windowpane; too sunny a position for orchids that do not like too much sunlight; not enough shade; spraying the plant in sunlight.
Remedy: protect the plants from too much sunlight.

Heat shock
Symptoms: irregularly formed, but clearly defined, yellowish, depressed spots on the upper- and undersides of leaves. The spots later turn brown and dry out.
Causes: collapse of leaf tissue due to too much heat in the case of a damaged root system or a position that is too dry.
Remedy: stand the plant in a cooler, moister but slightly shadier position.

Brown leaf spots; dying leaves
(see illustration, p. 32)
Cause: incorrect care
Remedy: remove dead leaves and dust the points where they were attached with antiseptic charcoal powder.

Concertina growth
Symptoms: the leaves do not unfold properly.
Causes: damaged roots because of "wet feet" (waterlogging). This often occurs when growing orchids in hydroculture.

Striking colours and patterns give the flowers of Odontoglossum hybrids their exotic appearance.

Remedy: cut off damaged roots, disinfect with charcoal powder and transfer to fresh compost.

Dry, brown leaf tips
(see illustration, p. 32)
Causes: air too dry; too high a concentration of salts in the compost through overfertilizing or using water that contains too much lime; waterlogging.
Remedy: increase humidity and rinse the compost under running water. Stop fertilizing for the time being. Repot the plant in the spring.

Light green or marbled leaves
Cause: magnesium or iron deficiency. Often occurs in *Cymbidium, Zygopetalum* and *Paphiopedilum.*
Remedy: a magnesium preparation, or add a combination of iron and magnesium to the water (ask at your local garden centre).

Red buds, falling buds, limp buds
Causes: lack of light; short-term low temperatures; not enough nutrients; roots in a bad state; often typical for certain species. Usually occurs in early to mid-winter. Often in *Phalaenopsis* in hydroculture if humus is left on roots when converting to hydroculture. Air containing ethylene (see p. 22) created by close proximity to fruit.
Remedy: treat the roots of plants in hydroculture. Otherwise stand the sick plant under a plant lamp for healing purposes (see p. 19).

Reluctance to flower

Causes: not taking account of the proper rest phases of the plant; in some species a lack of sufficient night-time drop in temperature; a position that is too warm; fertilizers containing too much nitrogen. This often occurs in *Paphiopedilum* species which require cool temperatures to trigger flowering.
Remedy: study the plant's growth cycle. The following year, care for the plant so that the proper flowering time is observed (see care, p. 17 and individual instructions for care, p. 39).

Pests

The pests that affect orchids are insects of the biting and sucking kind, as well as their larvae, and spiders that suck sap or eat the leaves and roots. This causes weakening or damage to the orchid to the point where it will die if nothing is done to put things right.

Aphids

(see illustration, right)
They will only occur on the young, soft shoots of orchids. These

Mistakes in care
Brown spots on leaves and leaf tips.

2-3-mm long insects establish themselves in dense colonies at the tips of shoots or around buds.
Symptoms: sticky leaves (honeydew). Deformation of shoots.
Causes: draughts, open windows,

or sitting in very dry, warm air.
Remedy: remove insects by hand and spray the plant with a plant protection agent. Repeat the procedure again in eight to ten days. Orchids grown in hydroculture can be treated with a systemic agent. In greenhouses, conservatories or

Pests
Left: aphids; right: scale insects.

even in plant windows, you can try employing gall midges and lacewing eggs, see p. 34).

Scale insects

(see illustration above)
Scale insects hide, along with their eggs, under a whitish-yellow to brownish layer of wax and are often discovered far too late. The larvae are minute, move very quickly and are generally not noticed at all. The plants most at risk are *Cattleya*, *Cymbidium*, *Dendrobium* and *Phalaenopsis*. The pests will tend to colonize leaves and pseudo-bulbs.
Symptoms: secretion of honeydew; formation of sooty mould; yellow spots on leaves; dropping leaves.
Cause: air too dry.
Remedy: increase humidity immediately. Scratch off scales with your fingernails or with a thin stick. Wipe down plants with a lukewarm soap solution or with cottonwool balls dipped in spirit. If this is all to no avail, spray the plant with a paraffin-based oil or try a leaf-shine spray.
Note: Generally, only hard-leafed orchids (e.g. *Dendrobium kingianum*) can cope with leaf-shine spray.

Mealy bugs

(see illustration, p. 33)
These belong in the same category as scale insects. Their favourite positions are leaf axils, the undersides of leaves and on bulbs.
Symptoms: whitish, woolly or cottonwool-like waxy excretions; crippled growth of plant.
Cause: air too dry.
Remedy: paint affected areas with alcohol. Increase humidity. If necessary, employ plant protection spray.

Red spider mites

(see illustration, p. 33)
These pests are the nightmare of all orchid growers who own greenhouses. Unfortunately, they occur quite often and tend to like *Cymbidium*, *Dendrobium*, *Paphiopedilum* and *Phalaenopsis*.
Symptoms: silvery, mottled leaves which turn yellow later on.
Cause: dry air.
Remedy: make sure the humidity is increased. Use the plastic bag method (see p. 35). Twice a week, spray the plant with lukewarm water during the morning. Spray with a special plant spray intended to combat spider mites. Employ predatory mites in greenhouses or conservatories (see p. 34).

Thrips

This 1-2 mm long, brownish-black insect has two pairs of folded, black and white wings. The almost invisible larvae tend to hide underneath leaves. Thrips damage the plant by sucking the sap from leaves, flowerbuds or flowers.
Symptoms: brownish spots on crippled flowers; deformed buds; the leaves look silvery, caused by air pockets in the puncture holes; brownish marks underneath the leaves; often black, shiny spots of excrement.

Cause: dry, heated air.
Remedy: spray with a suitable plant protection spray. Do not forget to spray underneath the leaves! Increase humidity immediately.

Cyclamen mites and root mites
Cyclamen mites do not often appear on orchids. They may suck the sap of buds or new leaf shoots of *Paphiopedilum*. Root mites attack weakened, sick plants and eat the roots from the inside out.
Symptoms: crippled growth of the buds, new shoots and leaf stalks; eaten roots.
Remedy: spray with an acaricide.

Diptera, Sciaridae
These are 4-7 mm long, black flies that tend to fly up at the slightest touch. Their larvae love humus-rich or peat-rich compost and if there is

Pests
Left: mealy bugs; right: red spider mites.

nothing else better to eat, they will devour orchid roots.
Symptoms: damaged roots; sickly plant.
Causes: transmitted from other indoor plants; importation from outside.
Remedy: Mafu or Vapona strips or sticky yellow tags. Insert yellow tags into the compost of individual pots.

Collembolae
These creatures are 1-3 mm long, look like white maggots and jump about. Generally they are useful as

they ensure the decomposition of dead parts of plants in the garden. In the confines of a flowerpot, however, they tend to consume the peaty particles in compost and then move on to attack the roots.
Symptoms: evidence of damage on the roots; crippled growth.
Cause: too much watering in the darker season of the year.
Remedy: during the mornings, rinse the compost several times in lukewarm water.

Slugs and snails
Slugs and snails often appear as night-time visitors in free-standing greenhouses. They are attracted by the humid warmth. As any gardener will tell you, they can inflict a great deal of damage with their voracious appetites.
Symptoms: eaten parts of plants; holes in leaves and bulbs; slime tracks.
Causes: carried in on orchids that have stood outside during the summer months.
Remedy: collect them, either early in the morning or in the evening. Sprinkle slug pellets.

Fungal diseases

In most cases, fungi are parasites which attack already weakened plants and they will only appear if the orchid has been subjected to much stress through dry air, lack of light, sunburn or other outside influences. Fungi will often colonize the holes bitten in plants by other pests. Orchids can be infested with terrestrial *Fusarium*, rusts and moulds. Bad ventilation encourages infestation.

Fusarium
Fusarium spores are always present and may be transported along with dust. They come up from the

ground to settle on the surface of the compost.
Symptoms: spots on leaves, crippled growth, decayed spots. Occurs most often in *Miltonia*, *Odontoglossum* and *Zygopetalum*.

Diseases
Left: leaf spots caused by virus attack; right: black mould.

Causes: "cold, wet feet"; too much fertilizer containing nitrogen; bad ventilation.
Remedy: remove diseased parts of the plant. Disinfect cut surfaces of the plant with charcoal powder. Dip the entire plant, including roots, in a fungicide and spray thoroughly with the same, then add fresh compost. Isolate the plant for the time being. Very badly infested plants will often not recover at all. As a natural measure, try spraying the entire plant with garlic tea (for recipe, see p. 34).

Cercospora
A harmful fungus that typically attacks *Dendrobium*.
Symptom: spotty leaves.
Cause: weakening of the plant through mistakes in care.
Remedy: as for *Fusarium*.

Orchid rust
This is a rare fungus which sometimes occurs in imported plants. *Cattleya*, *Epidendrum*, *Laelia* and *Oncidium* are particularly at risk.
Symptom: yellowish to rusty red spore colonies on the leaves.

Causes: humidity too high; infection in country of origin.
Remedy: isolate the plant. Remove all infested parts of the plant. Immerse the entire plant in a suitable protection agent and repot in fresh compost.

Rotting flowers
This is caused by the harmful fungus *Botrytis* which also attacks strawberries in gardens.
Symptom: spotty flowers.
Causes: too much nitrogen in fertilizers; draughts; leaves which remain wet for too long; infection from other indoor plants.
Remedy: remove affected parts of plants. Disinfect cut surfaces with charcoal powder. Spray plant with a suitable plant protection agent.

Black rot
(see illustration, p. 33)
Caused by *Pythium* and other species of fungi.
Cattleya, Laelicattleya and *Laelia* are particularly at risk.
It is generally young plants that are infested and which tend to tip over during the night.
Symptoms: weeping wounds along the edges of leaves and new shoots (soft rot); reddish spots on leaves; blackish-brown discoloration of the neck of the root; decaying patches on bulbs.
Causes: humidity too high; waterlogging; low temperatures.
Remedy: immediately remove all diseased parts of the plant. Disinfect cut surfaces with charcoal powder. Immerse the entire plant in fungicide and repot in fresh compost.

Bacteria

These are, of course, invisible to the naked eye and by the time symptoms are observed it is usually too late to do anything.

Fortunately, they are very rare on windowsills or in conservatories.
Symptoms: slimy, porridge-like, moist patches on leaves and bulbs; yellow, glassy-looking tissue.
Causes: infestation through water; wind-borne or carried in compost or from other plants.
Remedy: generally in vain. If infestation is mild, isolate the plant, remove all infested leaves and water frequently with garlic tea or a protection spray containing etheric oils.
My tip: Ask for advice from orchid experts in the case of rare or very precious plants.

Viruses

Orchid raisers dread viral diseases among their plants. *Cymbidium* and *Phalaenopsis* are particularly at risk. Fortunately, viral diseases, like bacterial diseases, are fairly rare.
Symptoms: crippled growth and discoloration in flowers; small black and brown spots (leaf spot viruses, see illustration, p. 33); striations on the leaves; purplish spots on *Cattleya* leaves.
Causes: infection through poor hygiene or ventilation or via insects.
Remedy: isolate infested plants at once and wait for a few days. Not every deformed flower or spotty leaf is infected with a virus. If infestation progresses rapidly, throw the plant away.

Useful insects

The following problems with pests can be combated by employing useful insects:
● predatory mites to control spider mites
● lacewings and gall midges to control aphids
● ichneumon flies to combat white fly

This practice is particularly successful in greenhouses, conservatories and windows conataining many plants. Useful insects can sometimes be obtained from garden centres and seed merchants.

Alternative control

Garlic tea to control fungi and bacteria
Crush one garlic clove, add it to 1 litre (1¾ pt) of water and bring to the boil. Allow it to cool and use as a preventive measure once a week by spraying it on plants or watering sick plants with the brew. Garlic contains fungicidal substances and antibacterial compounds which are still effective even when extremely diluted.

The plastic bag trick
The easiest, cheapest and most harmless way to get rid of spider mites is to create a "sauna". Water the infested plants well, then pour away any excess water. Place the pot inside a large, transparent plastic bag. Tie up the neck of the bag and leave the plant inside for one or two days. Use bags from dry cleaners for very tall *Vanda* or *Cymbidium* plants.

Other help

If you are not quite certain about your own diagnosis of a problem, you can always turn for advice to your local garden centre or phone your nearest orchid nursery or society.

Living with orchids
Orchids look particularly effective on a glass-topped table. This combination of plants contains a Phalaenopsis hybrid, Paphiopedilum and Ascocenda.

Successful propagation of orchids

The simplest method is vegetative propagation using parts of a growing plant. With this method, the offspring will be exact replicas of the parent plant. A much more complicated method is generative propagation, from seed, which goes hand in hand with the exciting possibility of raising a new cultivar. Just what the new young plants will look like is always a great surprise. Even beginners have managed to achieve some astonishing success using this method.

Vegetative propagation

This method of propagation involves taking rooted or unrooted, large or tiny parts of plants from a parent plant and then continuing to grow these parts in pots or test tubes. No pollination will influence the genetic material and thus the new plants will be exact replicas of the parent plant. Orchids can be vegetatively propagated in many different ways:

● by division (see illustration, p. 37)
● by cutting off small daughter plants (see illustration, p. 38); shoots or bulbs (see illustration, p. 37)
● by rooting shoots or cuttings (see illustrations, pp. 37 and 38)
● through meristem culture. This involves peeling a microscopically small part of a cell from a budding shoot and placing it in a test tube filled with a sterile nutrient solution. By constantly turning the test tube, a lump of tissue is formed that can be divided up into as many pieces as desired and cultivated further in another test tube with more nutrient solution. In this way, hundreds of identical plants (or clones) can be create from one original plant. This method cannot be used at home as it involves technical equipment only found in laboratories. I can, however, recommend the purchase of orchids propagated in this manner – called mericlone orchids. They are known to be highly resistant to disease (particularly to bacteria and viruses).

When is an orchid ready to propagate?

Very young or recently purchased flowering orchids are not suitable for vegetative propagation. However, you can go ahead with propagation from:
● plants that are several years old, large, completely healthy and strong
● orchids which are reluctant to flower and are quite old (often found in hybrids from several different genera, for example *Brassolaeliocattleya*.
● daughter plants which have formed by themselves on the parent plant and have produced rootlets (see illustration, p. 38)
● plants with overhanging bulbs that are on the point of dropping off
● orchids which automatically split into two or more pieces while you are repotting.

The right point

Orchids cannot be propagated at just any time. The best time is in the spring, during repotting or after flowering as the parts of the young plants will root better if they are able to grow on through the warm months with more light.

The importance of good hygiene

Any type of propagation is stressful for an orchid. During and after propagation, however, it is more vulnerable than at any other time to attack by disease-causing agents. Good hygiene is the best preventive measure.
● Before and after cutting, disinfect your scissors or knife with pure alcohol.
● Dust all cut surfaces or injured parts with antiseptic charcoal powder.
● Large cut surfaces may be treated prophylactically with a fungicide.
● Always allow cut surfaces to dry a little before planting the cutting in fresh compost.

Methods of vegetative propagation

The manner of propagation will depend on growth. Monopodial orchids with only one shoot (see p. 6) should be propagated in a different manner from sympodial orchids with several shoots (see p. 6). There are various different methods, some trickier than others.

Propagation from the division of monopodial orchids

Example: *Paphiopedilum*
If you remove the compost during the repotting of lady's slipper orchids, you will find that the rootstock automatically falls apart.

Propagation through division
Monopodial (one shoot) orchids often fall apart into two or more plants when the old compost is shaken out during repotting. You can then repot each plant individually.

Sympodial (several shoots) orchids are divided so that each new plant possesses at least three to five bulbs with leaves. The resulting pieces will only regenerate if they have these leaves; the bulbs only if they are fat and green.

NB: Never divide plants that do not have at least six strong, healthy shoots. Be careful when dividing. Torn sections will either not grow well or will not grow at all.

Propagation from the division of sympodial orchids

Example: *Cattleya* (see illustration bottom left)
You should only divide this plant if the part to be removed has at least three bulbs with leaves. For example, six single-row bulbs can be divided into two plants. In *Cymbidium*, however, leafless, plump bulbs can also be divided up.

Propagation from daughter plants

Example: *Phalaenopsis* (see illustration, p. 38)
Remove the daughter plants that have formed on the stalks of flowers – some growers maintain that these are formed through mistakes in care. As soon as they have formed their own rootlets, cut them off, together with a small portion of the stalk of the parent plant, and then fix the daughter plant to the surface of the compost with a wire clip.
My tip: A special growing paste can be obtained in the gardening trade which stimulates the formation and growth of daughter plants on flower stalks. The paste is applied to an "eye" on the stalk and the hormones contained in the paste trigger the formation of a daughter plant.

Propagation from cuttings

Propagation from the cuttings of monopodial orchids

Example: *Vanda* (see illustration below)
Cuttings for propagation can be taken from orchids that have grown too tall. To do this, cut off the uppermost part of the stem exactly beneath the aerial roots. Place the removed part of the plant in a very aerated, coarse bark compost.
Important: The parent plant must be at least 20 cm (8 in) tall if it is to recover from the procedure.
My tip: *Vanda* and *Dendrobium* may be propagated from daughter plants that grow on the end of an old flower stalk. Cut off the daughter plant about 2 cm (¼ in) below its aerial roots and place it in compost that is heat- and air-permeable.
Important: The aerial roots must not be too short.

Propagation from cuttings of sympodial orchids

Example: *Dendrobium* (see illustration, p. 38).
You can take cuttings from the stalks of this genus of orchids. Each cutting should be about 10-15 cm (4-6 in) long and possess four or five segments.

Monopodially growing species, like Aërides, Angraecum, Renanthera and Vanda, may be divided if they are older and healthy and have plenty of leaves and lots of aerial roots. Take the cutting at a level of about 20 cm (8 in), close beneath the aerial roots, and place the cut-off portion in a small pot. This cutting should form shoots after a few months. This is more difficult with Phalaenopsis!.

Propagation from daughter plants

Phalaenopsis often forms small plantlets on its flower stalks. These are well suited to propagation if they are removed together with a piece of stalk and fixed to the surface of some compost with a clip. They will quickly start growing on this moist, warm base. Daughter plants are also formed by Vanda and Dendrobium.

The pieces should be placed longways in sphagnum moss mixed with polystyrene flakes, and kept moist and warm.

Potting and care

The pots used should be small and the compost should consist of 50% polystyrene flakes as plenty of air will stimulate root formation. A mixture of *Meranti* (see p. 26) or equal parts of sphagnum moss and polystyrene is very good. Parts of plants that were already growing in compost (for example, divided bulbs) should not be placed any deeper in the compost than they were before. The cuttings of sympodial orchids should be bedded horizontally in compost. "Warm feet" and humid air will help to promote the formation of new roots and shoots. Stand the pots or bowls in a large, transparent plastic bag which should be tied tightly at the top. The moisture in the compost will be sufficient to keep them going and you will not need to water them. Placing the propagated plantlets on a heating pad is ideal. Even better still, stand the pots in a heatable propagation bed with a lid but without the plastic bag. Fill the bed with slightly moist peat beforehand.

Keep the lid on the device until new shoots have formed. With both methods, if condensation develops, air the container occasionally. As soon as fresh, green shoots appear, remove the plastic bag or lid and carry on as appropriate for the relevant species.

NB: You will now need some patience until the first flowers appear. Flowering maturity varies from one genus to another but you will, however, have to reckon with at least two to five years. In the meantime, the plant will grow leaves. It should be cared for in the same way as the parent plant.

Propagation from cuttings

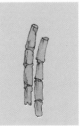

Some sympodial orchids, like Dendrobium, may be propagated from cuttings. Cut a strong, healthy shoot into sections of about 10-15 cm (4-6 in) long, which should all have at least three leaf knots. The pieces should be laid in a dish filled with moist sphagnum moss and kept warm and humid. If desired, the whole dish can be enclosed inside a plastic bag.

Generative propagation and raising

Propagation of orchids from seed is difficult, time-consuming and as exciting as taking part in a lottery. Whether you have "won" or not will not become obvious until the seedlings have flowered for the first time.

Pollination

The formation of seed is always preceded by pollination during which different genetic material is combined.

What plants can be crossed?

Successful pollination is possible between:

● two different plants of the same species
● two species of the same genus
● hybrids of one genus with hybrids of another
● hybrids with species.

Method

You will need a pointed stick or tweezers and two mature orchid flowers in full bloom.

● Using the stick or tweezers, remove the pollen from one flower. These male pollen carriers are usually situated behind a cap that has to be lifted up slightly.

- Place the pollen grains that stick to your pollination instrument on the female parts of the other flower. In many orchids this part is slightly sticky so that the pollen grains will not fall off (see illustration, p. 9).
- After pollination, attach a tag bearing the names of the parents to the stalk of the flower.
- After a few days (often just hours later) the pollinated flower will suddenly wither.
- The ovary will swell and, later, a capsule-shaped fruit is formed. This capsule must be allowed to ripen, which may be quick or slow depending on the species. These are a few average times:

Cattleya: 10-12 months
Cymbidium 11-14 months
Odontoglossum 7-10 months
Paphiopedilum 8-10 months
Phalaenopsis 4-10 months
Vanda 15-20 months

- The seeds are ripe when the capsule is brown at the top or generally appears pale. Now you can cut it off.

Sowing

If you want to try doing this yourself, you will need a proper seeding laboratory. Beginners usually send their harvested seed to a plant laboratory (ask a good orchid nursery) where the seed is treated under optimal conditions. If the seed is capable of germinating you will receive the seedlings back as pricked-out young plantlets in pots. You can then carry on growing the plantlets in a greenhouse or indoors in warm, humid, airy conditions.

NB: Depending on the species or genus, from three to six years may pass from the moment of pollination until the first flowers appear. Then the moment of truth will finally arrive and at last you will be able to see the result of your own raising attempts.

The most popular orchids – care and growing

The following pages present a selection of the most beautiful orchids, including exact descriptions, recommendations for varieties and much advice about care.

All of these orchids can be kept indoors and are easy to get hold of. They will be listed in current catalogues published by garden centres and nurseries and were all recommended to the author by orchid specialists for growing on windowsills.

Explanation of keywords

The first part of the name is always the botanical name of the genus, for example *Cattleya*. Beneath this is the common name if there is one. The introductory paragraph describes the orchid genus and gives a description of its appearance, lifestyle, special characteristics, etc. After this, you will find individual keywords with exact instructions on care.

Country of origin: this is important information for the correct care of the species. An orchid from the warm and humid Caribbean region will have quite different requirements with respect to temperature, light, humidity and water than an orchid that originates from the cool, moist, Andean mountain forests.

Temperature range: cool, temperate or warm. This division corresponds to growing positions in the original habitats of each plant. These are not exact, but rather

approximate values. Some genera are represented in only one temperature region, others in all three.

Flowering time: this indicates the main flowering season of a genus, species or hybrid. There is no indication here of how long the flower lasts or even of a possible secondary flowering. All statements are to be read as indications only, as the flowering time depends greatly on care and position. In many hybrids, the range of variation is so great that no definite flowering times can be given.

Colour of flowers: all colours that may occur within the orchid genus are mentioned.

Position: this gives indicators about light requirements as derived from the conditions in the country of origin of the plant.

Temperature: you will find information on summer and winter temperatures and on the relevant daytime and night-time temperatures.

Watering: this deals with proper care during watering, spraying and the vital necessity of humidity.

Fertilizing: gives information on when and how often you need to feed the plant.

Repotting: instructions on when and how often to repot a plant.

Compost: I recommend that beginners use special ready-made orchid compost. Generally, there is a reference to the relevant section on care (see p. 25).

Propagation: this indicates the method that is usually most successful for a particular genus.

Pests, diseases: problems typical to certain species are described here. More information on control can be found in the section on care (see p. 33).

My tip is a section in which I relate some of my own experiences or offer advice I have received from other orchid lovers and have tried out successfully myself.

Additional information:

The named species and hybrids were chosen according to attractiveness and ease of care. They represent a small selection from the huge kaleidoscope of internationally known orchids and their cultivars.

The species and hybrids of each genus have been listed according to their flowering times for a better overall view and ease of selection. If you use this information skilfully, you will be able to grow flowering orchids all year round on your windowsill.

An ideal plant for a hanging container
Coelogyne cristata is a vision in white and not very demanding in care.

The beautiful, two-coloured Cattleya bicolor.

Cattleya bowringiana will produce lots of flowers.

Cattleya

The flowers of *Cattleya* are conspicuous for their size, are very colourful and possess a striking lip. In addition to the 40-60 species, there are numerous attractive varieties and hybrids. Their noted ability to adapt, combined with great vitality in crossing has made *Cattleya* one of the most popular orchids.

In its countries of origin, *Cattleya* usually grows as an epiphyte on branches or trunks of trees. Two types of growth can be distinguished: one forms slender, flattened pseudo-bulbs with one leaf, the other develops club-shaped, often woody, pseudo-bulbs with two leaves. These are typical Brazilian *Cattleya*. Bud formation is conspicuous in all *Cattleya*. A spatha forms in the axils of the bulbs, which then develops into a bud. You can buy *Cattleya* species, *Cattleya* hybrids and even multigeneric hybrids (see p. 10), for example *Brassocattleya*, *Brassolaeliocattleya*, *Epicattleya*, *Potinara* and *Sophrolaeliocattleya*.

Countries of origin: Central and South America, Caribbean region.

Temperature range: temperate; warm, for example *Cattleya dowiana*, *Cattleya aclandiae*, *Cattleya schilleriana*.

Flowering time: varies, depending on species or variety (see p. 43).

Colour of flowers: pure white (so-called albinos), pink, violet, red, yellow.

Position: place in very bright position all year round but protect from direct sunlight. Ideal: an east- or west-facing window.

Temperature: during the summer and the vegetative period, warm (up to 25°C/77°F) and airy during the daytime. Important: there should be a drop in temperature of several degrees during the night. Some species and their hybrids can stand even more heat accompanied by increased humidity. During the winter, most species and hybrids make do with 18°C/64°F during the daytime and 14°C/57°F during the night.

Watering: according to demand during the summer; during the winter only enough to stop roots and bulbs drying out. Spray leaves frequently from late spring to mid-autumn to ensure adequate humidity.

Fertilizing: during the summer with every third watering; not at all during the winter.

Repotting: every two to three years. For plants that flower in spring and summer, after flowering; for autumn- and winter-flowering types, in early to mid-spring.

Laeliocattleya "Mibelle" has dainty flowers like a Laelia but should be cared for like a Cattleya.

Compost: see page 25.
Propagation: from division of bulbs (see p. 37).
Pests, diseases: fairly rare on account of tough pseudo-bulbs and leathery leaves. The main enemies are scale insects (see p. 32) but also watch out for ants which are attracted by the sticky secretions from the spatha and are often accompanied by aphids.
Special features: brown coloration of the sepals is typical of the species, also the formation of bast (phloem) on the bulbs, which serves to protect them from sunlight.
My tip: To ensure that your *Cattleya* flowers annually, you will need to stand the plant in a cooler position and reduce watering as soon as the shoot has matured. If you keep *Cattleya* too warm it will produce lots of shoots and form only leaves. You can act as something of a "midwife" during the opening of the flowers. Carefully cut open the protective sheath around the flowerbud with nail scissors to help the bud break through. Hold the bud up to the light to avoid injuring it.

Cattleya species
Spring-flowering:
C. amethystoglossa,
C. guttata, C. intermedia,
C. mossiae, C. skinneri
Summer-flowering:
C. aurantiaca, C. dowiana,
C. forbesii, C. gaskelliana,
C. harrisoniana,
C. intermedia, C. mendelii,
C. schilleriana
Autumn-flowering:
C. bicolor, C. boweringiana,
C. labiata, C. loddigesii
Winter-flowering: *C. bicolor,*
C. labiata, C. luteola,
C. percivaliana, C. trianae

Cattleya hybrids
Spring-flowering: "Bonnie Lisa", "La Tuilerie", "Lemforder Tricolor", "Moneymaker", "Shellie Compton"

Summer-flowering: "Princess Margaret", "Wichmanns Liebling"
Winter-flowering: "Edwin Hausermann"

Special features
White hybrids – summer-flowering: "Schwanendaunen"; winter-flowering: "David Bishop", "Karae Lyn Sugiyama Patrician", "Periwalker"
Yellow hybrids – spring-flowering: Hardyana "Clement Moore x Jane Helton", "Madame Dubarry Lemforde", "Rheinfels"
Scented hybrids – spring-flowering: "Amy Wakasugi Su Lin", "Robert Tan"; winter-flowering: "Edgar van Belle Safran"

Cymbidium flowers appear in a multitude of shapes, attractive colours and exotic patterning.

Cymbidium

The vigorous *Cymbidium* must be the foremost supplier of cut flowers among all orchids. Mainly originating in Thailand, thousands of flowering sprays are sold in flower markets all over the world, sought after for their extremely longlasting flowers and vast colour range. *Cymbidium* is thought to be represented by up to 50 or 60 species. They can be found in the most varied living conditions, from tropical rainforests right across the range of climatic zones to relatively dry regions. *Cymbidium* belongs among the terrestrial orchids, but some of them inhabit rocky terrain or even trees. Its name is derived from the Greek word *kymbos* which means boat or punt and this probably refers to the lip which curls up like the prow of a boat. Another characteristic of *Cymbidia* is thick, fleshy roots and the long, tough, strap-like leaves which usually grow out of oval pseudo-bulbs. The single flowers look as if they are made of wax and are very enduring. *Cymbydium* hybrids can be purchased in the gardening trade. Very popular are the standard types which grow very tall. They belong among the cold greenhouse plants and are splendid specimens for conservatories. The early-flowering types are more suited to indoors, particularly the miniature *Cymbidia* (see p. 45). These orchids had warmth-loving ancestors and will tolerate heated rooms. They grow to a maximum of 1 m (3 ft) and flower from autumn onwards.

Origin: tropical Asia, Australia.

Temperature range: temperate to warm, some cool.

Flowering time: varies depending on the species and hybrids.

Colour of flowers: creamy white, yellow, pink, green, red, orange, brown, violet.

Position: airy all year round, very bright and sunny. Standard types and older miniature *Cymbidia* in a very bright but not too sunny position outside from early summer to mid-autumn.

Temperature: during the summer, warm during the daytime; from mid- to late summer distinctly cooler at night. During the winter 20°C/68°F during the day; a little lower during the night – 10°C/50°F is sufficient for large hybrids at night; miniature *Cymbidia* should be kept no cooler than 15°C/59°F.

The photographs show Cymbidium hybrids:
1 Red Beauty "Wendy"
2 white hybrid with tiger-striped lip
3 "Starbright Capella"
4 "Vanguard"
5 green hybrid with spotted lip
6 "Sensation Chianti"
7 "Halleluja"
8 "Sylvia Muller Citronella"

Watering: from early spring to mid-autumn, plenty of water, but less in late autumn and winter. Make sure that humidity levels are high and mist frequently, even in winter.

Fertilizing: from early to mid-spring until the autumn, every four weeks.

Repotting: every two years during the spring. For spring- and winter-flowering types, after flowering is over.

Compost: see page 25.

Propagation: from division of bulbs (see p. 37), preferably when repotting (see p. 27).

Pests, diseases: spider mites if the air is not humid enough. Yellow-spotted, light-coloured leaves indicate a viral disease. As a preventive measure, isolate the plant and consult an expert.

My tip: Although *Cymbidia* are robust plants, they can be quite moody when it comes to the formation of new flowers. The prerequisites for flowering, in my experience, are lots of light and the correct temperature fluctuations during the run-up to flowering. For hybrids and those varieties that flower from early autumn to mid-winter, this should be done in late spring to early summer; in those that flower from late winter to late spring, it should be done in the period from late summer to mid-autumn. During these important periods, the plants require plenty of warmth during the daytime and plenty of fresh cool air during the night.

Cymbidium species
Spring-flowering:
C. devonianum,
C. lowianum
Summer-flowering:
C. aloifolium
Autumn-flowering:
C. giganteum
Winter-flowering:
C. eburneum
Cybidium standard types (hybrids)
Spring-flowering: "Jungfrau Münz", "Trade Winds", "Clan Steward"
Autumn-flowering: "Baltic Dream", "Drama Shooting Star", "Magpie"
Winter-flowering: "Advent Charm", "Kurun Magie"

Miniature *Cymbidia*
Winter/spring-flowering:
"Agnes Norton Show-off", "Dag Oleste", "Excalibur", "Mary Pinchess Del Rey", "Miniatures Delight" (hanging plant), "Minneken Pink Tower", "Lemforde Surprise" (scented)

Cymbidium hybrid "Cassiopeia".

45

Dendrobium densiflorum.

Dendrobium

Dendrobia form the second largest orchid genus. There are several hundred species. A characteristic feature of many Dendrobia is the long pipe-like pseudo-bulbs which look almost like bamboo shoots. These stalks often consist of several segments and the flowers develop from the joins or even on leafless shoots from the previous year. The inflorescence is a raceme, garland-like or an umbel. In their countries of origin, Dendrobia live high up in trees, a fact that is echoed in their name (Greek: dendros = tree, bios = life). While the warmth-loving, pink Dendrobium phalaenopsis and its hybrids have become known for their longlasting cut flowers, it is more often the cool-loving species and cultivars that are offered for sale for growing in pots, for example the spring-flowering Dendrobium nobile and its hybrids. I can recommend Dendrobium pierardii, Dendrobium crepidatum and Dendrobium kingianum for beginners.

Important: Always ask about the relevant temperature range when purchasing Dendrobia.

Origin: Asia, Malaysia and Australia.

Temperature range: cool, temperate and warm.

Flowering time: mainly spring and winter; some in summer or even in autumn.

Colour of flowers: white (usually with a blush of pink or violet), bright pink, pink, red (from light to dark), violet, yellow, orange, cream.

Position: bright all year round. Protect from direct sunlight during spring and summer.

Temperature: Cool species: during the summer 15-18°C/59-64°F during the daytime, and around 13°C/55 F at night. During the winter around 13°C/55°F or above during the daytime and around 10°C/50°F at night. Temperate species: during the summer around 23°C/73°F during the daytime, cooler at night. During the winter, 16°C/61°F in the daytime and around 12°C/54°F at night. Warm species: during the summer up to 30°C/86°F in the daytime, only 20°C/68°F at night. During the winter, 22°C/72°F in the daytime, 18°C/64°F at night. Dendrobium nobile hybrids should be kept warm during the summer and during the autumn/winter at about 10°C/50°F to encourage flowers.

Watering: high humidity during the summer. Water abundantly during early spring to early autumn. Cool and temperate species should be kept almost dry during autumn and winter. Spray frequently, but only during the mornings. Warmth-loving Dendrobia should be kept in moist conditions all year round.

Dendrobium parishii closely resembles Dendrobium nobile.

Dendrobium minax is widely distributed on the Moluccan islands.

Fertilizing: from early spring to early autumn, fortnightly.

Repotting: every two years after flowering. Use small pots or small baskets for hanging plants.

Compost: see page 25.

Propagation: from daughter plants (see p. 38), division of pseudo-bulbs (see p. 37) or from parts of plants (see p. 38).

Pests, diseases: rare. If kept outdoors, watch out for snails which like to hide in the dense foliage of Dendrobium.

Special features: some Dendrobia lose their leaves, others continue to flower from old bulbs, so do not be hasty in throwing old plants away!

My tip: From early summer onwards, I hang my Dendrobium kingianum outside in the garden in a very bright, but not sunny, position sheltered from the wind. From early autumn onwards, I move the plant into full sunlight. The difference between daytime and night-time temperatures triggers the ripening of shoots and the formation of flowers.

Dendrobium species for a cool and temperate climate
Spring-flowering:
D. agregatum,
D. chrysotoxum,
D. crepidatum,
D. densiflorum,
D. jamesianum,
D. kingianum, D. nobile,
D. parishii, D. pierardii
Summer-flowering:
D. densiflorum
Autumn/winter-flowering:
D. phalaenopsis

Scented Dendrobium species
Spring-flowering:
D. primulinum,
D. speciosum,
D. superbum

Dendrobium hybrids for warm positions
Spring-flowering: "Doreen x Pale Face", "Garnet Beauty", "Indigo", "May Neal"
Note: I care for my Dendrobium kingianum in exactly the same way as my Coelogyne cristata (see photos, pp. 10 and 40/41).

During the winter it is placed in cool conditions on the windowsill of an unheated room; during the summer it spends time in the garden in a cool, moist, semi-shady place. I keep it constantly moist from spring to mid-autumn and fertilize it once a month. It is watered less during the autumn. The flower shoots appear as spike-like formations from early winter onwards and then transform themselves into elegant, hanging sprays of flowers during early spring.

Laelia purpurata is the national flower of Brazil.

Laeliocattleya hybrids have intensely coloured flowers.

Laelia

Lealia are very closely related to *Cattleya*. They are cared for in the same way and often crossed with each other. This genus, consisting of about 50 species, enchants the onlooker with the fiery shades of its flowers. In their countries of origin, *Laelia* are mainly epiphytic. There are also lithophytic species. The latter are sometimes called stone *Laelia* and are well worth trying by beginners, for example the cinnabar red *Laelia cinnabarina. Laelia pumila*, with its 10-cm (4 in) flowers is very attractive. *Laelia purpurata*, the national flower of Brazil, is a proud beauty with purple-lipped flowers. And if you happen to be looking for an intense orange orchid, *Laelia harpophylla* has just what you need.

Origin: tropical America.
Temperature range: temperate, some a little cooler.
Flowering time: varies depending on the species.
Colour of flowers: red, orange, yellow, white and violet.
Position: bright to semi-shady.
Temperature: during spring and summer 18-24°C/64-75°F during the daytime; during the night-time and during autumn/winter about 4°C lower (57-68°F).
Watering: during the summer, according to demand; during the winter only enough water to keep the plant from shrinking. Ensure there is enough humidity.
Fertilizing: with every third watering during the growth period.
Repotting: every two to three years.
Compost: see page 25.
Propagation: from division of bulbs (see p. 37).
Pests, diseases: watch out for stagnant air. *Laelia* will not take kindly to these conditions.

The photographs show *Laeliocattleya* hybrids:
1 white with a yellow column
2 cream-coloured
3 lemon yellow
4 "Culminari Recital"

Laelia species
Spring-flowering:
L. cinnabarina, L. purpurata
Summer-flowering:
L. crispa
Autumn-flowering:
L. autumnalis, L. pumila
Winter-flowering:
L. anceps, L. autumnalis, L. harpophylla

Laeliocattleya
Spring-flowering: *L. "Alma Wichmann"*
Winter-flowering: *L. "Max und Moritz", L. "Wintermarchen"*

Miltonia (Miltoniopsis) "Robert Strauss" flowers mainly during the spring.

Miltonia

Miltonia can be roughly divided into two groups. One group, which originates mainly from Brazil, can stand more warmth and is, therefore, more suited to indoor care. These are the species of the actual genus *Miltonia*. The other group comprises orchids which thrive in the misty forests of the Andes and require cool, moist air all year round. These are the "pansy orchids" which are now assigned to their own genus *Miltoniopsis*. The genus *Miltonia* includes approximately 15 species, inclusive of the *Miltoniopsis* species. These plants live as epiphytes and usually possess light green, flattened pseudo-bulbs with two or three narrow leaves, or only one leaf in the case of *Miltoniopsis*. The flowers always form at the base of the youngest pseudo-bulbs.

Origin: South America.
Temperature range: temperate or cool, depending on the species.
Flowering time: summer/autumn and all year round.
Colour of the flowers: multi-coloured, often white with red or pink, orange with dark brown.
Position: bright all year round but not sunny. Will also tolerate semi-shade.
Temperature: during the summer not above 25°C/77°F; during the winter around 20°C/68°F and 15-18°C/59-64°F at night.
Watering; keep evenly moist; water sparingly during the winter. Ensure high humidity.
Fertilizing: during the spring and summer every three weeks in very low doses.
Repotting: if at all, in the autumn or spring.
Compost: see page 25.
Propagation: from division of the bulbs while repotting (see p. 37).
Pests, diseases: due mainly to mistakes in care. A slight red discoloration of leaves may indicate a position that is too bright.
My tip: *Miltonia* are not entirely easy to look after.

The roots may get burned by salts from fertilizers or may decay if too much water is given. Although they require high humidity, you will still have to be careful not to overdo things when misting.

Miltonia species for the temperate climate
Summer/autumn-flowering: *M. clowesii*, *M. flavescens*, *M. spectabilis*

Miltonia hybrids
Summer/autumn-flowering: "Anneliese Weber", "Celle", "Fritz Wichmann", "Gascogne x Hamburg", "Goodale Moir Golden Wonder", "Hambühren", "Koala", "Pink Frill", "Rouge California Plum"

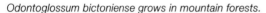

Odontoglossum bictoniense grows in mountain forests.　　*Multigeneric hybrids of Odontoglossum.*

Odontoglossum

Most of the approximately 100 species are beauties from cool mountain forests where they occur at levels of 1,500-3,000 m (4,920-9,800 ft) and may even be subject to short periods of frosty temperatures. This orchid genus received its name because of its unusual flower which sometimes sports a tooth-like appendage at the base of the lip (Greek: *odonto* = tooth, *glossa* = tongue). The pseudo-bulbs are egg-shaped and flat, bear one to three leaves at the tips and form upward-pointing raceme-like inflorescences at their base. Recommended for the beginner: *Odontoglossum grande* (more recently renamed *Rossioglossum grande*), *Odontoglossum bictoniense*, *Odontoglossum pulchellum* (smells of lily-of-the-valley), *Odontoglossum crispum* and its varieties, for example "Star of Columbia".

Many of these species are used for raising hybrids and multi-generic hybrids because of their attractive inflorescences and their almost legendary ability to adapt.

The best-known are:
Vuylstekeara: from *Odontoglossum* x *Cochlioda* x *Miltonia*
Wilsonara: from *Odontoglossum* x *Cochlioda* x *Oncidium*
Odontioda: from *Odontoglossum* x *Cochlioda*
Ondontocidium: from *Odontoglossum* x *Oncidium*
Odontonia: from *Odontoglossum* x *Miltonia*

Origin: Central and South America.
Temperature range: cool to slightly temperate.
Flowering time: autumn to spring.
Colour of flowers: mainly yellow with tiger stripes or spotted, white with pink or red.
Position: bright to semi-shady. East-, west- or north-facing windows. South-facing window during the winter.

The photographs show:
1 *Vuylstekeara* "Cambria"
2 *Vuylstekeara* "Cambria Plush"
3 *Odontonia* "Marie Noel"
4 *Odontonia* "Burkhard Wedringen"

Temperature: 20-24°C/68-75°F during summer; 14°C/57°F during winter. Slightly higher for plants that require more temperate conditions.
Watering: keep at a constant level of moisture during the growth period. During the winter water only enough to prevent the compost and the bulbs from drying out. Ensure high humidity.
Fertilizing: from early to late summer, fortnightly.

Vuylstekeara "Cambria Lensing's Favourite".

Fertilizing the leaves will prevent the compost and roots from becoming harmed by salts.
Repotting: every two to three years during the autumn or in the spring.
Compost: see page 25.
Propagation: by cutting off bulbs (see p. 37).
Pests, diseases: usually only due to very severe mistakes in care. "Concertina" leaves occur if humidity is not high enough (see. p. 31).
My tip: If you have a garden, hang your *Odontoglossum* in a tree with open foliage from early summer onwards. Do not forget to water it if the weather is hot and dry. If the summer turns out

mainly rainy, however, it is probably better to take the plant indoors again to prevent the compost going mouldy. The plant should be allowed to soak up plenty of sunlight during early autumn. This will encourage flower formation and maturing of the bulbs. From mid-autumn onwards, move the orchid back indoors, for example into a cool conservatory. If there is sufficient light, the plant will form reliable flowerbuds for the following season.

Odontoglossum species
Spring-flowering:
O. cariniferum (slightly temperate), *O. pulchellum,*

O. rossii
Autumn-flowering:
O. bictoniense (slightly temperate)
Winter-flowering:
O. crispum
Rossioglossum species (slightly temperate)
Autumn/winter-flowering:
R. grande, R. insleayi, R. williamsianum.

Odontoglossum hybrids
Flowering time all year round: "Anneliese Rothenberger", "Burghard Holm", "Gudrun Hambühren", "Hans Koch", "Star of Columbia"

Multigeneric hybrids
Odontioda "Coronation",
Odontioda "Feuerkugel",
Odontonia "Burghard

Wedringen",
Odontonia "Lulli Menuett",
Odontonia "Marie Noël",
Odontonia "Polka",
Odontocidium "Tiger Hambühren",
Vuylstekeara "Cambria",
Vuylstekeara "Cambria Lensin's Favourite",
Vuylstekeara "Cambria Plush", *Vuylstekeara* "Edna Stamperland", *Vuylstekeara* "Hambühren",
Wilsonara "Hambühren Stern", *Wilsonara* "Tigersette Lemforde"

Oncidium

The fiery, flame-coloured *Oncidium papilo* once earned *Oncidia* the common name of "butterfly" orchid. However, this orchid is no longer considered to be a genuine *Oncidium* by most botanists, but has now been placed in its own genus *Psychopsis*, just like its close relative *Oncidium kramerianum*. This genus, with about a hundred representatives, occurs in the most varied temperature zones and is also found in many forms: with large or small pseudo-bulbs, and with narrow or broad, fleshy or tough, hard leaves. Its inflorescences consist of delicate single flowers. This graceful orchid genus owes its name to the callus-like, warty appendages at the base of the lip (from Greek: *oncos* = callus-like mass). The individual flowers are often striped or flecked. The first plant – an *Oncidium flexuosum* – arrived in Europe from a range of mountains in Brazil in 1818. Today, more than 50 species are available in the trade. It is very important to know the particular temperature range in order to provide the correct conditions. Always remember to ask when purchasing these plants!

Oncidium forbesii was discovered in the Organ mountain range in Brazil in 1837.

Small flowers and wonderful scent: Oncidium ornithorhynchum.

Oncidium "Susan Kaufmann" – a fiery beauty.

Origin: subtropical and tropical America, Caribbean.
Temperature range: temperate, some cool or warm.
Flowering time: varies, depending on the species.
Colour of flowers: yellow, brown, but also pink, red and white in various combinations of colours.
Position: bright to semi-shady, no direct sunlight. Exception: during the winter.
Temperature: warm during the summer, cooling off at night. Temperate *Oncidia* 15°C/59°F in the daytime during the winter; warmth-loving ones around 20°C/68°F.
Watering: keep constantly

slightly moist from the beginning of the growth period onwards. Water just enough to prevent the pseudo-bulbs and the leaves from wilting during the winter. Ensure high humidity but be careful with misting during the winter and spring. New foliage will tend to become mouldy rather quickly.
Fertilizing: every three weeks during the growth period.
Repotting: towards the end of the rest period when required, and when roots and new shoots begin to grow.
Propagation: divide bulbs when repotting. Do not divide up into groups that are too small (see p. 37).

Compost: see page 25.
Pests, diseases: these only occur if serious mistakes in care are made.
My tip: Do not cut off inflorescences of *Oncidium kramerianum* or *Oncidium papilio* after flowering. New buds will develop on the same stalks during the following year.

Oncidium species (temperate zone)
Spring-flowering:
O. leucochilum,
O. sphacelatum
Summer-flowering:
O. carthagenense,
O. concolor, O. flexuosum
Autumn-flowering:
O. forbesii,
O. ornithorhynchum (scented), *O. varicosum*

Winter-flowering:
O. tigrinum

Oncidium species (warm zone)
Summer/autumn-flowering:
O. papilio, O. kramerianum.

Oncidium hybrids (temperate zone)
"Afternoon Delight", "Goldrausch", "Jorge Verboonen", "Rogersii", "Rotkappchen", "Thilo"

Oncidium hybrids (warm zone)
"Golden Cascade"

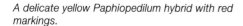

A delicate yellow Paphiopedilum hybrid with red markings.

Paphiopedilum hybrids are more resilient than pure species.

Paphiopedilum lady's slipper orchids

There are just over 60 species in Asia – and nowhere else. The number of hybrids is much greater. The orchid lover should only attempt to obtain cultivated lady's slipper plants in order to preserve the wild forms in their natural habitats. The cultivated forms have a great advantage, anyway, in that they are much tougher and grow better. Lady's slippers are mainly terrestrial, although a few are also lithophytic and epiphytic. They live in both the lowest levels of the jungle and up to levels of

2,000 m/6,500 ft. Most of them, however, are to be found in monsoon regions with alternating climatic phases. The inhabitants of cooler regions usually possess fresh green leaves, those in warmer areas have marbled leaves. Each leaf rosette only ever produces one single flower shoot. After flowering, only leaf rosettes will grow out of the leaf axils.

The first lady's slipper orchid, a *Paphiopedilum insigne*, arrived in Europe from the Himalayas in 1819.

Origin: tropical and subtropical Asia.

Temperature range: warm to temperate, more rarely cool.

Flowering time: varies, according to species or hybrid.

Colour of flowers: white, yellow, green, brown, purple; flecked or tiger-striped.

Position: semi-shady during the summer, bright during the winter, but never sunny.

Temperature: indoor temperatures all year round, cooler at night. Around 25°C/77°F during the daytime in the summer; around 15°C/59°F during the night in winter. During early autumn, after the shoots have finished forming, keep them cooler for two to three weeks at night and sunny during the daytime.

Watering: ensure that the plants are moderately but evenly moist. Do not water until the compost has dried out. Water moderately and only at midday during the winter. Keep humidity at high levels. Mist the leaves frequently.

Fertilizing: mid-spring to early autumn, every three weeks.

Repotting: every two years and only if the compost has become dense and hard or develops a fusty smell.

Compost: see page 25.

Propagation: from division (see p. 37). Lady's slipper orchids thrive as a clump and will grow more splendidly every year if left undivided.

The photographs show:
1 *Paphiopedilum bellatulum*
2 rust red *Paphiopedilum* hybrid
3 *Paphiopedilum insigne*
4 pure yellow *Paphiopedilum* hybrid

Pests, diseases:
infestation with spider mites and scale insects is possible. Decay of buds, leaves and roots through waterlogging.
My tip: Lady's slipper orchids love tiny pinches of lime. I always give my specimens a mixture derived from loess containing calcium oxide, tissue-building silicic acid and many trace elements. One knife-tip of this substance in 1 litre (1¾ pt) of water is quite sufficient.

Paphiopedilum species
Spring-flowering:
P. barbatum, P. bellatulum, P. hirsutissimum, P. sukhakulii

Summer-flowering:
P. callosum
Autumn-flowering:
P. concolor, P. fairrieanum, P. spicerianum, P. sukhakulii
Winter-flowering:
P. insigne, P. venustum, P. villosum.

Paphiopedilum hybrids
Autumn/winter flowering:
"Aladdin", "China Girl", "Goliath", "Kehler", "King Arthur", "Lemförde Novelty", "Maudiae"

In Europe since 1885: Paphiopedilum callosum from South-east Asia.

Paphiopedilum sukhakulii grows in sandy loam in Thailand.

Phalaenopsis hybrids flower nearly all year round.

Dainty flowers of Doritaenopsis "Malibu Queen".

Phalaenopsis
Malaya flower, moth
orchid

These elegant flowers look just like moths floating through the air. It is no wonder the Dutch botanist Blume came up with this common name. He found the first specimen in this genus of approximately 50 species in 1825 and called it *Phalaenopsis* (from Greek: *phalaina* – nocturnal moth and *opsis* – appearance). *Phalaenopsis* orchids are either epiphytic on trees or lithophytic on rocks and steep, mossy banks. They occur in tropical Asia up to a height of 4,000 m/13,100 ft and are accustomed to shady,

humid positions. They have not developed pseudo-bulbs as they originate from regions with fairly constant temperatures. Instead, they form many roots which cling to everything within close proximity and are extremely hard to detach. The leaves of these orchids are fleshy and fairly broad. In plants cared for under optimal conditions, the flowers appear nearly all year round. Although *Phalaenopsis* flowers appear to be as fragile as priceless bone china, they are not at all hard to care for. In fact, this is considered to be the ideal indoor orchid. Various species and hybrids, as

well as crosses with other genera, are all available in the trade. The robust, star-like forms which first appeared during the 1950s are still extremely popular. Well-known multigeneric hybrids include:
Asconopsis: from *Ascocentrum* x *Phalaenopsis*
Doritaenopsis: from *Doritis* x *Phalaenopsis*.
Renanthopsis: from *Renanthera* x *Phalaenopsis*
Origin: India, South-east Asia, Indonesia, the Philippines, Northern Australia.
Temperature range: warm.
Flowering time: all year.
Colour of flowers: white, red, pink, violet, yellow,

brown, green, golden, tiger-striped, dotted.
Position: semi-shady during the summer, bright during the winter but never, ever sunny.
Temperature: warm all year round (20-22°C/68-72°F during the daytime, never below 18°C/64°F during the night); warmer during the summer. During the autumn, keep them cooler for four to six weeks (around 16°C/61°F) to encourage flower formation.
Watering: keep moderately moist all year round. The compost should never be allowed to dry out completely but should always be slightly dry before the next watering.

se only soft, lukewarm
ater. Never water the
eart of the plant as this
rings the danger of decay.
pray the leaves often.
lake sure humidity is high
articularly for
halaenopsis species,
lthough the hybrids have
dapted to drier indoor
onditions.

ertilizing: every fortnight
uring the plant's growth
hase.

epotting: every two years
uring the spring. Do not
amage the sensitive roots.

ompost: see page 25.

ropagation: from
aughter plants which
ccasionally form on the
ower stalks (see
ustration, p. 38).

ests, diseases: fungal
seases from
verwatering; scale insects
the position is too dry;
lling buds in a position
at is too dark; at risk
om slugs and snails in a
reenhouse.

pecial features:
halaenopsis requires
lenty of air around its
oots. This means that you
ust definitely avoid
aterlogging around the
oots. Choose a very
oarse, air- and water-
ermeable compost when
epotting. Possibly choose
askets instead of pots.

ly tip: Phalaenopsis may
orm two or three lots of
owers on the same shoots
the flower stalk is cut off
bove the third or fourth
not in the stalk before
owering is quite over.

The photographs show:
1 "Mambo"
2 red-spotted hybrid
3 hybrid with slender petals
4 "Cassandra"
5 "Hokuspokus"
6 delicate yellow hybrid
7 pink hybrid
8 "Rudolf Baudistel"

Phalaenopsis species
Spring-flowering:
P. lueddemanniana,
P. sanderiana,
P. schilleriana, P. stuartiana.
Summer-flowering:
P. lueddemanniana,
P. violacea.
Autumn-flowering:
P. amabilis.
Recommended:
P. amboiensis which flowers
from spring to autumn.

Phalaenopsis hybrids
Flowering all year round:
"Bernstein", "Bolero",
"Bronze Maiden" (scented),
"Canary", "Eisvogel", "Elsa
Muenz", "Golden Sands",
"Goldfliegen, "Grace Palm",
"Haller Spatz", "Hello Dolly",
"How Lucky", "Julia Reuter
Darling", "Lemförder Tiger",
Lemförder Super Violet",
"Lipperose", "Mambo",
"Mildred's Baby",
"Morgenröte",
"Niedersachsen", "Rose
Satin", "Schneeglanz",
"Schone von Celle",
"Unnarose", "Zauberrose",
"Zauberrot"

Phalaenopsis-Doritis crosses
Autumn-flowering:
Doritaenopsis "Fuchsia
Princess", *Doritaenopsis*
"Malibu Queen",
Doritaenopsis "Mem.
Clarence Schubert"

There are countless Phalaenopsis hybrids.

The pleasantly scented Vanda tricolor is also called Vanda suaveolens.

Vanda

Some of the 40 existing *Vanda* species are epiphytic in their countries of origin. The strap-shaped, leathery leaves are set on in regular double rows or sometimes arranged like roof tiles on a long stem. The flowers appear in upright inflorescences that grow sideways out of the leaf axils. *Vandas* rarely grow taller than 120 cm (48 in) in a greenhouse, conservatory or flower window. The most beautiful species is the strictly protected *Vanda coerulea*. Its flowers are an incomparable shade of blue that otherwise never occurs in orchids or any other flower. Multicoloured *Vanda tricolor* spreads a strong scent.

As well as the large-flowering *Vanda* hybrids, other species are also for sale in specialist orchid nurseries. Crosses with *Ascocentrum* are recommended for use on windowsills as they remain small.

Origin: tropical Asia.
Temperature range: temperate to warm.
Flowering time: varies, depending on species or variety.
Colour of flowers: cream, pink, orange red, pale lilac, blue, violet.
Position: as bright and sunny as possible all year round.

Temperature: around 18-20°C/64-68°F in the daytime during the winter; above 25°C/77°F during the summer. Always a little cooler at night. *V. coerulea, V. cristata* and *V. kimballiana* should be kept a little cooler.
Watering: from late spring to early autumn, while the plant is growing, water plentifully and spray daily, including aerial roots. Water sparingly in winter and do not spray.
Fertilizing: every fortnight during spring and summer, low doses.
Repotting: only if the pot is too small. As a rule, every three years.
Compost: see page 25.
Propagation: from division or from shoots (see p. 37).
Pests, diseases: falling buds if the winter position is too cool. Lack of light causes reluctance to flower.
My tip: It flourishes with its aerial roots dangling over the edge of the pot.

Vanda species
Autumn/winter-flowering: *V. coerulea, V. kimballiana, V. tricolor*
Spring/summer-flowering: *V. cristata, V. sanderiana*

Vanda hybrids
Spring-flowering: "Nelly Morley", "Blaue Donau" Summer-flowering: "Onomea", "Rose Davies" Winter-flowering: "Rothschildiana"

Zygopetalum

When living rooms were still being heating with coal or wood-burning stoves and the area around a window remained fairly cool, the 60-70 cm (24-28 in) tall *Zygopetalum* used to be a popular potplant. The first two species, *Zygopetalum crinitum* and *Zygopetalum mackaii*, arrived in Britain between 1826 and 1829. Sir William Hooker first mentioned this genus in the *Botanical Magazine* in 1827. The genus includes about 30 species, most of which originate from Brazil. They form egg-shaped pseudo-bulbs with two or more narrow, lance-shaped leaves. The flowers appear laterally along the pseudo-bulbs and are often strikingly patterned or coloured. Nearly all species form numerous thick roots and grow best in roomy pots. Their peculiar name is derived from Greek and refers to the thickened callus at the base of the lip which holds the petals together like a horse collar (Greek: *zygon* = horse collar, *petalon* = petal).
Origin: South America.
Temperature range: temperate.
Flowering time: winter.
Colour of flowers: brown, pink, red, green and violet.
Position: bright to semi-shady.
Temperature: room temperature. Cooler and airier during the winter (15-18°C/59-64°F).
Watering: keep constantly moist all year round. Make sure there is plenty of humidity but do not spray the leaves if possible as they will develop spots.
Fertilizing: in low doses every fortnight from spring to autumn.
Repotting: every year as *Zygopetalum* does not like its roots to be tightly confined.
Compost: see page 25.
Propagation: from the division of bulbs bearing leaves (see p. 37).
Pests, diseases: root decay or fungal infections of the leaves if too much moisture is present. Stagnant air will encourage infestation with thrips and red spider mites.
My tip: The inflorescences may become quite heavy and I recommend propping them up with sticks to give them extra security.

Zygopetalum species
Winter-flowering:
Z. crinitum or *Z. mackaii* (which are considered to be the same). Also *Z. intermedium*.

Zygopetalum hybrids
"Artur Elle", "John Banks", "Seagulls Landing"

Something a bit different: Zygopetalum "Artur Elle".

59

Index

Words in **bold** indicate illustrations.

Index

Index

Cover photographs
Front cover: *Miniature cymbidium hybrid, cattleya, Dendrobium biggibum (Cooktown orchid).*
Inside front cover: *orchid window with Phalaenopsis and Vanda hybrids, Oncidium (Psychopsis) kramerianum, Cymbidium devonianum, Dendrobium densiflorum and Ascocentrum curvifolium.*
Inside back cover: *three different Odontoglossum hybrids.*
Back cover: *Thelymitra ixioides (Sun orchid).*

© 1992 Gräfe und Unzer GmbH, Munich

Reprinted 1998, 1999, 2000, 2001

This edition published 1995 by
Merehurst Limited
Ferry House, 51-57 Lacy Road,
Putney, London SW15 1PR

ISBN 1 85391 433 9

English text copyright ©
Merehurst Limited 1995
Translated by Astrid Mick
Edited by Lesley Young
Design and typesetting by Paul Cooper
Printed in Hong Kong by Wing King Tong

Odontoglossum hybrid flowers with striking markings.

Photographic acknowledgements
Cover photography by L. Rose.
Burda/Stork: p. 20, 48 left, 54 left,
54 Nos. 1 and 4, 57 No. 4,
Eisenbeiss: p. 24, 25, 40/41, 42
right, 42 left, 47 left, 47 right, 48
No. 2, 50 left, 53 left, 55 top, 56
right, 58, 59, C4 bottom left and
bottom right. Luckel: p. 7, 49.
Wetterwald: p. 52. Stork: all other
photos.